PRAISE FOR

Just a Girl

"This is a critical book that all corporations should study in order to evolve their companies into a place where women want to work. Lucinda Jackson tells it like it is, and her takeaways and review of legal precedents are relevant to all women and men who work in corporations."

—SILVIA GARRIGO, Global Vice President,
Millicom International

"Riveting, searing, and personal—readers of this book will be inspired to redouble society's efforts to create a more fair and equitable culture for both women and men."

—CHERYL KARPOWICZ, Senior Vice President,
Ecology and Environment, Inc.

"Lucinda Jackson attains shero status as she chronicles her triumph over sexual harassment that is ever present as air. A corporate scientist and academic, Jackson compellingly weaves her personal story with society's awakening and progress toward addressing this scourge."

—ANDREA JARRELL, author of *I'm the One Who Got Away:
A Memoir*

"This powerful memoir will help other women, in spite of antifemale adversity, overcome pain, self-blame, and shame. It will be especially beneficial to vulnerable young women as they try to make their way in science, technology, engineering and math (STEM)."

—BEVERLY ENGEL, LMFT, bestselling author of *I'm Saying No!
Standing Up Against Sexual Assault, Sexual Harassment,
and Sexual Pressure*

JUST A GIRL

JUST A GIRL

Growing Up Female and Ambitious

LUCINDA JACKSON

Published 2019
Printed in the United States of America
ISBN: 978-1-63152-662-6
ISBN: 978-1-63152-663-3
Library of Congress Control Number: 2019906547

For information, address:
She Writes Press
1569 Solano Ave #546
Berkeley, CA 94707

She Writes Press is a division of SparkPoint Studio, LLC.

Book design by Stacey Aaronson

To Deborah and Linda and all women like us who have been put down and harassed. I'm sorry it happened to you. I believe you, it's not your fault, and it's time for us to be free.

CONTENTS

Prologue | 1
Introduction | 3

PART I: 1950s-1960s

Chapter 1: Heavy Messages | 19
Chapter 2: Keep Us Silent | 43

PART II: 1970s-1980s

Chapter 3: Keep Us Down | 63
Chapter 4: Keep Us Out | 97
Chapter 5: Upping the Game | 142

PART III: 1990s-2010s

Chapter 6: The Corporate Ladder | 165
Chapter 7: Boy Children | 187
Chapter 8: The Cycle of Harassment | 205

Conclusion: Stay and Speak Up | 235
Epilogue: Freedom | 245
Notes | 251
Acknowledgments | 261
About the Author | 263

PROLOGUE

AS I RAN MY FINGERS OVER THE SHINY GOLD TUBES OF lipsticks, I didn't think much about the man at the other end of the display counter. I noticed him, as he seemed out of place among all the girls and women in the makeup section of Cornet's, our favorite five-and-dime store. But he was an older man, dad-like, probably just looking for something nice for his daughter or his wife.

I hummed and fidgeted, ecstatic just to be there at the mall. My sister, Deborah, three years older than my nine years, and I had gone there with friends. It was a big deal, because my mother had never let us go shopping on our own before. In my favorite turquoise-and-green matching Bermuda shorts-and-top outfit, clutching a stained white purse with a chipped chain handle, I felt so sophisticated. I had found the purse in a garbage can in a public bathroom—probably somebody had stolen the contents and dumped it there—but I didn't care. I strutted a little and snapped my fingers a few times when I wore it slung over my shoulder, jazzed, since my mother wouldn't let me buy a purse yet because she said I was too young. As we filed into Cornet's, I was especially thrilled that we were going in to look at makeup, because, of course, I didn't wear any.

My sister and friends drifted down the aisle, and I was alone looking at the treasure trove—mascara, rouge, compacts, red lipsticks. Then I felt a poke in my side, peered down, and saw a huge purple sausage jutting out of the father-man's dark pants and butting up against me. My mind raced: *How did he move down the aisle and end up next to me? Where did he come from? Is this a penis?* I'd seen my brother's penis in the bathtub, but it never looked scary and threatening like this. I froze. Poke, poke—he jabbed me again. And again.

What's happening? What's this nice man doing? Why's he doing this? My blood iced up in my veins. Panic rushed through my body. Away from my friends, I realized I was his target, the deer separated from the herd.

I gasped, survival mode kicking in, and bolted down the aisle and out into the mall. My stomach swirled, ready to throw up. Why had he chosen me? What was wrong with me? Why would someone do that to me?

I found my sister and friends and fell sobbing into their arms. My baby blue-framed glasses fogged up with tears as I choked out my story.

"How horrible for you!" they said. "What should we do? Ick, ick! Let's get out of here!" We slunk out of the mall and held on to our secret.

I feel ill talking about it even now, after almost sixty years; that betrayal, such a brief act, ruined my childhood foray. What I didn't realize then was that I'd been sexually harassed for the first time.

INTRODUCTION

IT TOOK ME DECADES TO UNDERSTAND, BUT NOW I KNOW why there aren't many women in science, technology, engineering, and math (STEM) fields in America's colleges and universities. I also know why only a dismally small number of women hold higher-level positions in corporate America, the world of big companies in the United States: It's because men, especially men with power, prevent women from entering and remaining in these fields and companies. They don't want us there, whether it's in a math class, college, academia, government, or a corporate job. They do what they can to keep us out or, if we get in, to make us quit. Men profit from the current system, since they control wealth and authority. They have fun in their man world, and they want it all to themselves.

I know what I'm talking about. I spent more than eight years working in science in a university environment and almost forty years in male-dominated professions in the corporate world. As I entered that world in the 1970s, I saw that men there had special benefits: camaraderie, power, and money. They joked, exchanged exploits, talked about sports and women. Each of them had his own office with a wooden desk and carpeting. They had expense accounts, company cars, and airline travel, during which they flirted with female flight attendants. They drank at bars, convened for golf after meetings, and fished together on the weekends.

They were well paid and wore nice suits. They had creative jobs and got respect and promotions. They decided how it was going to be. They had it made.

When I was young, I saw the jobs available to me as a woman: waitress, motel maid, bank teller, secretary, sales clerk, or cashier. And if I went to college, maybe I could be an elementary-school teacher, executive secretary, or nurse. I understood that these were all lower-paid and more repetitive jobs, with little opportunity to advance. No travel, no big desk in your own office. I would never be in charge.

Still, I wanted what men had. I sought the power and advantages of the man world. Riveted by its glamour, I hammered away in high school, chose science—a men's major—in college, and later managed to secure a "man job" as a field research biologist. I danced crazily and sang around my apartment when I got that first job offer, as science was not only a ticket to the man world but also my love.

But there were problems. I was sexually harassed—a lot. The harassers' occupation wasn't a factor. I was harassed by teachers, professors, doctors, bosses, colleagues, and random strangers. Geographical location didn't matter. The harassment occurred all over the United States and all over the world—Asia, Africa, Europe, and so on. The harassment cropped up in schools and universities; in part-time jobs on farms, in restaurants, and at hotels; and in career positions in major organizations—so setting didn't matter either. And the harassment happened at multiple corporations, so it wasn't limited to just one bad company I happened to work for—it was at all of them.

Sexual harassment went like this for me: Knuckled

down and upbeat, I was aflame with my work, intrigued with math and science and their practical application in the real world. I explored, questioned, and was productive in my research, willing to do any job, no matter how dirty or difficult it became in the weedy fields or the sticky-hot greenhouse. Then a man—my colleague, my boss, or client—would approach and say, "Why don't you and I get to know each other better?" in a sexual tone. He could deny it later by saying, "Can't a guy even be friendly?" but he and I both knew what he meant.

Or he'd sidle up too close and say, "You look pretty today, sweetheart," as he flung an arm around my shoulder.

Or, "I hear you're from California. Want to take a hot tub with me? Isn't that what they do in California?"

Oh no. Every time, my heart sank, my chest tightened, and a dizzying wave of dread came over me. I knew as clearly as if the men had said it out loud that I was not there because I was smart, dedicated, or talented. I knew they didn't want me in their midst at all, except as a plaything. They didn't really welcome me as a scientist—I was an annoyance, an outcast. I knew someone with power over me was threatening my right to be there.

Heart palpitating, I'd stutter, "Oh, uh, gee, thanks, but . . . I'm sorry, I have a . . . boyfriend" (a lie and a line that never worked to deter them). I was always afraid I'd say the wrong thing. I knew I couldn't be rude; I had to be polite. I floundered for words that just wouldn't come and ended up with a nervous giggle and twitch to cover my anxiety and the cold sweat starting to drip down my back.

For me, white, heterosexual men were the worst sexual

harassment offenders. Minority men were a different story. In general, they could relate to my situation, because often they were the only black, Asian, or gay man in the room, just as I was the only woman. And they faced considerable discrimination and isolation as well—although they did get invited on the fishing trips, while I didn't. Minority men were, like I was, trying to find their place, to be included, to be part of the man gang. They often became my friends and confidants, although usually they would not speak up for me, since they were fighting their own battles against the classic WASP, heterosexual boys' club.

The whole fifty years of my career were a difficult time to be a working woman in America. I lived through the glacial evolution of laws—from the beginning of my work life, in the 1960s, when there were no laws at all against sexual harassment, until the 2010s, when a few protective measures were in place.

What is sexual harassment? The official definition is "unwelcome sexual advances, requests for sexual favors, and other verbal or physical conduct of a sexual nature that tends to create a hostile or offensive work environment." But, in reality, sexual harassment is about the bullying of a weaker person by someone dominant. Historically, men are the players with the power and women are in the weaker position. I know men get harassed, too, but almost 85 percent of the sexual harassment charges reported each year to the Equal Employment Opportunity Commission (EEOC) from 2010 to 2017 were filed by women. [1]

Sexual harassment has been going on extensively and for a long time, yet it didn't even get a legal name until 1975.

For years before that, US courts dismissed it as a "private matter" that had nothing to do with work—when these incidents even made it to court at all. The belief was that sexual advances by men could happen anywhere—the workplace, a deserted park, or someone's living room—so sexual harassment was not the responsibility of corporations when it happened in their offices, and they definitely weren't liable.

Still, studies show that up to 90 percent of women in the workplace have experienced sexual harassment, depending on the industry [2], and I bet in the sciences it's closer to 100 percent. A 2014 study reported that 64 percent of female scientists surveyed had been sexually harassed during fieldwork alone. [3] But it's our nasty little secret, since few women talk about it. Why don't we? Out of shame? Fear? I know women for whom I am the first one they have told about their "incident," and that was as long as thirty years ago. Even Barbara Boxer, the confident and strong former United States Senator of California, confessed in her 2016 book about a creepy episode involving her college professor's extorting her for sex in exchange for grades. [4] Prior to her book, she hadn't told anyone except her husband about it. Some women I know have never even told their spouses.

Sexual harassment is complicated and can be subtle. It's not usually rape or physical abuse or some huge moment but something smaller, yet it can be devastating when it's iterative and cumulative. It weighs on us over and over again until we truly believe we are worth nothing. It can be vague, not every day, not violent—just a periodic reminder that we should not be here, we are not worthy, and they just want us to go away.

After the fact, sexual harassment causes feelings of humiliation and shame. We become afraid that if we tell anyone, there will be terrible repercussions for *us*, not our harassers. It's easy to blame ourselves, to think that something we did *made* them harass us. All of this can lead to depression and loss of self-confidence. The traumatizing effects of sexual harassment linger for decades. Most women my age have at least one story that strikes a nerve: "Guess what happened to me?" Even if the harassment happened decades ago, it's still emotional. Tears, anguish, and anger result from even speaking of it, which most of us don't. Instead, we keep silent.

While I was enduring my own forms of sexual harassment, I was in the dark about legal changes going on in America. The social context was hard to realize, too, because I was right in the middle of it, living it. I found myself swamped with work, trying to figure everything out, and orchestrating my active life. But it's important in retrospect to view what transpired against the backdrop of legal and social events that were taking place at the same time.

I knew there was a law prohibiting race-based discrimination in the workplace, because I heard about the 1964 Civil Rights Act, but I didn't know then that the Civil Rights Act pertained to women, too. Maybe it was the word "his" in the actual text that threw me off. The law asserts that it is "unlawful employment practice" for an employer "to fail or refuse to hire or to discharge any individual, or otherwise to discriminate against any individual with respect to *his* [my italics] compensation, terms, conditions or privileges or employment, because of such individual's race, color, religion, sex, or national origin." Apparently, the word "sex" was added at the eleventh hour in an amendment to the Act by Representative Howard W. Smith (D-VA). I saw the document myself while browsing the Library of Congress one day with one of my sons. Up on a plain wooden wall, the amendment, neatly typed up and stamped "O.K. Accepted" on February 8, 1964, read "insert the word 'sex'" in five places on four different pages. After my audible gasp, which caused other visitors to look my way, I motioned my son over to share the moment. I hugged him to my side as I stood there with a teary face for this small token that protected us women from employment discrimination. The gender part of the Civil Rights Act wasn't widely advertised, and someone like me hadn't even heard about Smith's amendment. Some say that Smith was trying to kill the bill by adding "sex" as kind of a joke, but the word remained and the bill passed anyway.

In the early years of my career, I certainly also had not heard of Title VII of the Civil Rights Act, which created the Equal Employment Opportunity Commission (EEOC) in 1964 to implement the law. No one ever talked about Title VII, and it wasn't publicly announced to any young girls in the 1960s. I finally learned about the EEOC in the early 1970s, and only in a negative light: from men talking about how that organization forced them to work with women. We were kept in the dark about the new legal rights that gave women protection from discrimination in the workplace.

In truth, equal employment opportunity (EEO) was a real nightmare for me. Male colleagues said, "You know,

Lucinda, EEO is the only reason you were hired. You aren't really qualified; you're only here because the company has to comply with a stupid law. The company lowered its standards to hire women."

In the 1970s, right when I was entering the science workforce, there was an immense backlash against women breaking into traditionally male jobs. It was permissible for women to be nurses, teachers, or assistants, but taking a man's job was unthinkable. Men used harassment as a weapon to frustrate us and block our efforts to participate in jobs they believed belonged to them. The idea was to make women feel so unwelcome that we would leave of our own accord. There were efforts to humiliate and demean us, whether through direct sexual assault, innuendos, or flat-out lies. We suffered in a macho culture from abuses we had to put up with at the hands of men.

Sexual harassment is the main weapon men use to keep women silent, down, and out. The world needs more women scientists and more women in academia and corporations, but achieving that goal calls for fundamental shifts in the way women are treated and the way men behave. We need a whole movement, a new culture. Women are speaking up more, which is wonderful. We need that, plus laws and training. But we further require real social change to produce liberated men and women, because harassment and discrimination absolutely still exist.

My first hope is that, after reading this book, anyone who has experienced female harassment and debasement, like I did, and feels bad, sad, and mad about it, will take the time to heal and move on. My aim is that those who have been harassed will feel better. I want women to recognize that they are not alone, that someone believes them and knows their harassment was not their fault. I visualize these women recovered and taking action. Some women say they didn't face harassment problems in college and the work-place—they were just one of the guys or shrugged it off. But what about the rest of us, who didn't know we could speak up, who were, in fact, programmed not to? We didn't know about any laws protecting us, and even if we did, we were too afraid to say anything. We were just trying to get by, just making our way in the world. I'm speaking here for those women, the ones who took it and suffered because they had no voice and little confidence.

I dream that all harassed women will come out of the closet and give up their secrets because, by speaking out together, we can kill this beast that has made us feel ashamed and guilty. More than 75 percent of women ha-rassed in the workplace never say a word or make a formal complaint to a supervisor, manager, or union representative. [5] I want this story to embolden us all to keep on keepin' on—to be instrumental in changing this statistic, pressing the issue, supporting other women, raising liberated boys and girls, and avoiding dropping out. It may be hard, but we women must join and remain in the academic and corporate worlds to help those institutions transform.

To men and boys who might read this book: I have myriad wonderful male figures in my life—my husband, three sons, a grandson, two nephews, and many male friends. I hope, with new inspiration, you will start a boys' and men's liberation movement. I still see boys not allowed to feel their emotions or cry. I see men hampered in the workplace from becoming full fathers and partners because of old stereotypes. This needs to change. I hope this story will help you understand how bad sexual harassment makes someone feel, so that you won't do it, so that you'll teach your sons not to do it and teach your daughters to fight it. No—I repeat, *no*—woman asks to be sexually harassed. Let me go on—even if that woman is dressed up and wearing low-cut, tight clothes and lots of makeup, she does *not* want to be demeaned, abused, taunted, demoralized, or shamed. She might like your attention, a smile, or a nice compliment, but she is *not* looking for trouble or your insults. Especially if you're married or in a position of power over her, you're not what she wants. Despite what many men say—"I was just trying to be nice"—they know the difference between a compliment and a come-on.

I also wrote this book for history. Unfortunately, the stories of workplace sexual harassment I hear today are the same as those I experienced fifty years ago. It's discouraging that, even amid the social and legal changes that have happened, we have not made more progress. I want to tell the history of this era in American work culture, based on my own thoughts and memories about what happened during those times, in order for understanding and transformation to occur. I've used studies and research to back up what I'm saying, to offer a wider view—but much of this is what happened to me personally over decades.

If you are an older woman, please tell your story about sexual harassment in our generation so that no one forgets the history of this scourge. All women, girls, men, and boys should know how pervasive sexual harassment has been and still is in the United States, and how negatively it impacts women's self-image and ability to function—and, thus, the productivity of a nation. Let's make our statements part of the literature on this subject, so everyone knows that there were not only a few of us who had this problem—that sexual harassment was, and remains, widespread. I believe our struggles need to be documented for posterity so that our experiences are not swept away into the past.

My wish is that this book contributes to breaking the historical cycle of events that leads to sexual harassment in America. The cycle includes parents, teachers, college professors, and employers. It can and must be broken. I speak to parents about raising liberating boys and girls. To those in academic and corporate America: I want you to realize how this affliction in our society negatively affects careers and productivity, and how it suppresses our country as a whole. I advocate for a remodel of the culture of universities and particularly of corporate America, since corporations rule in the United States and in most of the world. This is a call to action to revolutionize our academic and corporate cultures into kinder, more diverse entities that ensure women can join, contribute, and stay. This reform will encourage more women to choose STEM fields in college and finish their degree. It will allow more women to join corporate America and not quit to find a safer environment. If you are in a position of power in a university or corporation, I want you to see how unproductive sexual harassment is and how it is holding your organization back.

Last, to be honest, this book is also for me. Writing it

was a way to explain to myself why I was such a target for so much sexual harassment. I felt ashamed for a long time, alone in my silence and ignorance. I had to go back in time to understand how, beginning as a female child of the 1950s, I was indoctrinated to feel inferior to men. As a young woman, I was gullible, innocent, and naive. I always thought people had my best interests at heart and that everyone meant well. I wasn't beautiful, sexy, or particularly feminine. I didn't wear makeup, have my nails done, or sport long, fluffy hair; I was kind of skinny and athletic. We were told that men had natural sexual desires that had to be met, but there were women more attractive than I who didn't seem to get the same grief I did, and I always wondered why that was. If male sexual desires and needs were the drivers of sexual harassment, why didn't the men around me pick the prettier women?

I put off writing this book for a long time, primarily because I concluded that the harassment I encountered was all my fault. I feared that I would sound promiscuous and immoral in parts of this story—and I'm sure you can tell by what I'm saying here that I still suffer from victim guilt. Part of sexual harassment is making the victim believe it is her fault, and I fell for that for many years.

I learned later that self-blame is common for sexually harassed women, and it's taken me this long to reconcile myself to the knowledge that the events in my life were not a result of my wrongdoing. But even as I wrote this, I found myself cringing and castigating myself. I sensed I would sound like a fool who deserved everything she got. I dredged up many excuses for not speaking up. I was waiting for:

- My kids to grow up so I didn't have to be concerned about their shock or judgment.
- My husband to die so he wouldn't be disgusted by me (but when he read this book, I discovered he felt only sorrow and anger, not disgust, and I'm glad he's not dead).
- Retirement from the corporate world so I wouldn't have to worry about anyone calling me a liar and a slut, or worry about my résumé or a promotion.
- New laws that would declare nondisparagement agreements unenforceable. I wasn't sure, but I thought I'd signed something when I left these workplaces that swore me to silence regarding anything negative about the companies. Nondisparagement agreements are often in the news now and are seen as coercive, as they silence victims of sexual harassment, sexual discrimination, and age discrimination and allow these wrongs to persist.
- My harassers, many of whom are still alive, to die so they couldn't come back to "get" me or sue me.

This stuff is not easy to talk about. Remembering those degrading incidents makes them real all over again. As I started writing, my inner devil told me I was a real loser, a big downer, a buzzkill. Each time I sat down to write, my heart rate sped up and I grew sweaty and short of breath. I couldn't continue at all for a while—there was just too much flooding back inside my head and heart. Then I went to a workshop by renowned memoirist Mary Karr in San

Miguel de Allende, Mexico, and I got a chance to ask her how she does it—talk about things that are really painful. She encouraged me to treat the situation as though I were going through a divorce—take care of myself, get massages, go for walks. [6] That helped.

My story of a vulnerable young woman growing up in science and corporate America starts when I was a small girl with a fire in my belly who lived in a time when that fire was extinguished at every turn. I ran into one obstacle after another as I constantly faced sexual harassment. There are all sorts of books about accomplished corporate women who are confident, powerful, one of the boys, and for whom everything goes well. But that was not my life. Although I rose to the upper levels of the corporate world and managed hundreds of employees and billions of dollars across the globe, I was always scratching along, trying to make my way in a hostile, anti-female world, struggling to make sense of what was happening. I am a successful executive, but I want to relate, in plain language, a personal account of the price I paid.

PART I

1950s–1960s

one

~⌒

HEAVY MESSAGES

SHORTLY AFTER MY PENIS EXPERIENCE AT THE MALL, AN obscene phone caller started bothering my sister and me. He'd call our house and begin by asking, "What are your names? How old are you girls?" We'd answer his questions politely, as we'd been trained to do. Then he'd say, "I want to put my penis between your legs. I have a hard penis just for you, and I want you to touch it. Would you do that?" and escalate to "I want to meet you in person near your house."

As he spoke, we kept our ears tight to the phone, wide-eyed and silent. If he asked us a question, we responded, murmuring yes or no, even though the urge to hang up was strong.

He usually wanted to talk to my sister and asked for her by name, but one time when he called and I was about to go get her, he said in a low voice, "No, I want you."

I digested this as, *He wants* me? *I'm nobody, just a little girl. I thought he liked my sister better. But maybe I'm somebody if this man now wants me, instead of her.* I remained on the phone and allowed him to carry on his sexual monologue. I somehow knew I couldn't tell anyone about it. It rankled me my whole life. It came back to me whenever someone started saying things to me that I didn't like, but I found myself unable to hang up the phone or walk out of the room, thinking that would be too rude or that somehow the offending person was in charge. I would freeze up and take it and then feel shame and regret that I hadn't acted.

As an adult, I started looking back on my childhood, with the help of various therapists, to see what messages I had received as a girl from important people in my life that had filled me with self-doubt, susceptibility, and guilt. Even though it hurt, I gathered that delving into my past would shed light on why I had encountered ongoing sexual harassment, starting at such an early age.

As a young girl in the 1950s, I loved any kind of competition. I always kept track of who got the top score in every game, race, and school test. My diary at eight years old boasted, "We played Clue, I won. We played hopscotch, I won. We had a test, I got 100."

An early reader and studious from a young age, I loved the library and combed the stacks on a weekly basis. I excelled in school (straight A's always!), sports, and all the games—kickball, hide-and-seek, dodgeball, roller skating, four square, basketball, freeze tag. I raced all the boys and often won, and was the fastest runner of all the girls. At the end of the school day, I rushed home, flung off my school dress, and pulled on my blue jean shorts with pockets, where I kept my jackknife and magnifying glass. I headed out, my thumbs tucked into my shorts, to the vacant lot down the street. There, I studied ants under my magnifying glass (even sometimes trying to burn them, I confess) and dissected twigs and plants with my knife to see what was inside. I spent as much time as I could exploring up on Terrace Hill behind our house. So absorbed was I in nature and all its mysteries, I frequently lost track of time and got in trouble when, toward dark, my mother didn't know where I was. But I was a budding scientist, a tomboy, an outdoor girl who loved spinning on the monkey bars on the play-

JUST A GIRL | 21

ground until I had blisters behind my knees, not caring that the boys taunted, "We can see your underpants!" while they purposely stood beneath the bars as the skirt I was required to wear swished up.

That young self-confidence quickly diminished as I got older. By the time I was nine, it was clear that I should be subservient to males—a sentiment weekly reinforced with the messages in my family's favorite TV show, *Father Knows Best*, in which the man was all-knowing, and the wife and girls were dingbats. I learned in school that underachieving boys got rewarded more and got away with more than smart girls, as teachers defended their behavior by saying "boys will be boys." I don't recall ever hearing "girls will be girls" as an excuse for our behavior.

Though there were plenty of other voices telling me this, too, it was mainly my father who imbued me with the idea that girls were auxiliary and should be submissive to boys. When I was nine, he told me, "You shouldn't beat the boys; they won't like losing to a girl." I slowed down so that I wouldn't win when I raced them.

He also told me, "You know, Cindy, boys don't like girls who are smarter than they are. If you want boys to like you, you have to cut out that crap."

In deference to his teachings, I secretly erased the solutions to my math problems in elementary school and did them over so the boys wouldn't know how quickly I'd finished, sitting at my rickety wooden desk with my arm covering my work so no one would see. I purposely wrote the wrong answer to a problem so I wouldn't stand out as smart and therefore become unpopular, especially with the boys. As I'd learned from my father, the most important goal was for them to like me.

Despite all the messages I was receiving at home, I

couldn't completely let myself go academically. It just wasn't my nature. In secret, I labored over all my homework each night, studied and read on the weekends, pushed myself, and wanted to excel. I saw that I could get approval from my adult teachers, so I started going the extra mile to get the best grade and their praise. But none of these efforts impressed my father.

"Cindy, all you really need to do is learn how to cook. That's the most important thing, because it's what men like in a woman," he informed me.

He also told me, "Girls don't need to go to college; it's a waste of time. They just need to learn how to take care of a man. College is stupid anyway, and doubly unnecessary and worthless for girls. Don't bother with it."

My father's friend Dan visited, and one day, while he leered at me as I crept by in the living room, he added, "What you should do is become a 'kept' woman. I was a kept man for an older woman one summer on a sailing boat, and it was the best time of my life."

My father agreed. This was the only piece of career advice I received from him.

MY CHILDHOOD IN the 1950s appeared idyllic in many ways, with forts and games and playmates in small-town San Luis Obispo, California. My parents had distinct, traditional roles typical of that era. As a child, I studied my mother slaving away at home in her little housedress and apron, while my father, in his business suit and tie, went off in the only car to his professor job. He came home, had a highball, read the paper, and listened to dreary classical music while my mother, still working, rushed around to put dinner on the table. Not just any dinner, mind you, but one that fit all the criteria that he demanded, all from scratch: meat, potatoes, vegetables, salad, and homemade apple pie for dessert. On the weekends, she still worked, trying to do something with us kids, like a craft project or a drive to the beach so we could swim and buy penny candy. Meanwhile, my father played tennis and golf and went fishing, and we never saw him. He had summers off, since he was a teacher, but it was my mother who packed my two siblings and me into the old Pontiac and drove us to our grandparents' house in Seattle so that my father could have three months to himself.

It was clear to me from early on that my parents' relationship was lopsided. My father dominated and my mother submitted. He was an angry rebel who scoffed at convention, got himself dismissed from his college professorships, and had fights at work because he wouldn't toe the line. Her biggest ambition was to be a respected "faculty wife," so she was devastated that she lost that status when her husband was fired from two universities.

He was always purposely embarrassing her. I heard a constant refrain of "Oh, Harry!" throughout my childhood, whenever he did something unorthodox. One Sunday when we were dressed up, marching along in a park, my father began complaining that he was hot and sweaty. He pulled out his jackknife, reached down, and cut off his slacks up to his thighs, mortifying my mother in her flowery dress and dainty heels. He donned skimpy red running shorts and a ragged pink T-shirt that said HANG 10 on it for tennis, when she craved the pressed, all-white Wimbledon look. At my mother's fancy dinner table, adorned with a white tablecloth and cloth napkins, he would intentionally plunk down a milk carton and a beer on it to spoil the effect. We three kids would all freeze, waiting to see what would happen. My heart started to pound every time I knew there was a standoff. He would catch her eye, daring her to object. It was an act of defiance, an insult to my mother, a power play. As she glanced away, her subjugation shot right down into my own gut, like it was meant for me, too, as the milk carton stayed and my father won.

Our car was a 1930s humpbacked Pontiac that he had painted himself with chalky light blue house paint that came off on my clothes whenever I balanced on its running boards. My mother constantly denounced it. Even as a child, I knew it was old and not as good as the cars of my friends' families, and I reddened every time a friend came over and saw that painted car sitting in our driveway. But the Pontiac remained, just like the milk carton.

My mother certainly could not have bought her own car, one she liked. She told me, "I have no money; it all belongs to your dad. If I need anything for myself or you kids, I have to ask him for it. But I don't like to ask him, because he usually gets mad."

I remember thinking, *How can she live this way? I don't want to have to ask anybody for anything when I get to be her age.* It was then that the seeds of determination never to be like my mother began to germinate inside me.

Sundays especially creeped me out. My mother would be busy with housework and laundry and special Sunday dinner preparation and trying to pay attention to her kids, and my father would start pacing around the house. Around three o'clock, he would announce, "Ellie, it's time for us to take a nap."

She'd reluctantly put down her work or stop the game she was playing with us and obediently go into their bedroom. She always looked back at us; even as a kid, I could see an uncertain look in her eyes—a look that let me know something was wrong. But she would always go. It turned my stomach. I didn't know exactly what they were doing in there, but I knew it wasn't good from Mom's viewpoint. From what I saw, she was his slave and his concubine, someone who kowtowed to him in all ways, and recalling it still nauseates me.

ONE DAY MY sister and I strolled home from school, accidentally slamming the front door behind us as we arrived in the front entry, but our mother was nowhere to be seen. She was always home—where was she?

"Mom?" we called, alarm rising in us. Then we heard a soft weeping and moaning from a dim corner of the living room, where the drapes were unexpectedly drawn on the sunny California day.

We peered around into the darkness and saw her crumpled on the rug. She wailed, "Daddy hit me."

I couldn't see all of her clearly, only her knees tucked under her homemade housedress with the ever-present apron over it, and her curly hair hanging over her chest. But it wasn't the sight of her that sent chills down my body. It was her choked voice and that awful, unbearable wounded-animal sound. My whole image of my mother was smashed up and spit back out. I now saw her as someone small and weak who couldn't help herself, let alone me.

Of course, my sister and I didn't know what to do, so we hightailed it out of there, leaving her alone. None of us ever said another word about the incident, but it left me with a terror that kept me awake at night in my suburban twin bed. As I lay there, I wondered over and over, *What if Dad gets angry enough and hits me? Why does he get to do that to Mom? I feel sorry for her, but why doesn't she do something about it? Who will protect me against him?* The seedlings of my will never to let what happened to my mother happen to me were continuing to take root. She was my antihero—I vowed never to be like her, to be just the opposite.

DURING MY FEW, rare glimpses into my father's work world, I noticed his engineering students admiring him; his office at the college, with a big desk, windows, and tools; and his classroom, filled with machines. It all looked like fun. I didn't want my mother's life of fear, abuse, subservience, and catering to him. I wanted his life—my own money, a job where I was important, away from the house. This was definitely the beginning of my interest in the man world, which looked like a better deal to me, although, because I was so conditioned to see myself as powerless and deficient, I would have to struggle to obtain it.

At home, we all continued to operate under an umbrella of fear of making my father mad. On weekend mornings, he wanted to sleep in, so the house needed to be silent. We'd get up early, as kids do, to play with our tinker toys and Muffie dolls. Then we'd hear his whistle—a high-pitched reed whistle, decorated in yellow and red swirls, small and evil, which he kept in his nightstand—and freeze with anxiety, careful not to breathe or clang any blocks together, as we awaited our fate. My father had impressed on us that after that whistle blew, something really bad would happen to us if we didn't shut up. He had to charge out only one time in his baggy boxer shorts, swearing and yelling, to make me perpetually afraid of his anger and fearful of how bad it could get if I made him mad. Not if *he got* mad, but if *I made him* mad.

There was a tape running in my head that went something like this: *Never make a man mad. Don't cross him, don't challenge him, don't make a fuss; keep quiet and out of sight.* This conditioning plagued me into my adult years, when my biggest fear was that a man would get mad at me. This fear caused me not to speak up, not to say what was in my head. I tried to shield myself from men's presumed anger by being sweet and quiet. Years later, I said to a friend at the office, "We shouldn't mention our idea for an alternative approach to this problem; it might make Henry mad."

A lightning bolt hit me when she said, "So what?"

This idea that making a man mad maybe wasn't the end of the world was reinforced when a counselor I sought out for help later in life said to me, "What's the worst that could happen?"

I replied, "He would get mad."

"So what?" she said. It took me hearing this many times to realize that I had been relying on those old tapes in my head way past their usefulness. Training from childhood dies hard. I wasn't going to get hit or shamed or silenced if I spoke out as a grown-up—and if I did, so what? I was no longer a child. As an adult, I could do something about it.

I NEVER DID anything with my father. I remember striding along in our neighborhood with him by myself only once, one summer night. My best friend, Tracy, asked me to spend the night on that warm Southern California evening when I was five. I beamed and jiggled all day as my excitement for my first sleepover mounted. I packed my brother's old green sleeping bag with the checkered flannel lining, my favorite doll, Susie, and my stuffed animals Flower and Teddy, and headed down Sylvia Court, past the five small tract houses that made up our cul-de-sac. As usual, I breathed in the freshly mown lawn scent that I liked and, since I couldn't help it, the faint stink of an incinerator burning garbage. I marched past the yards, full with kids from each house playing outside on the grass and sidewalk, toward Tracy's, one block away.

"I'm spending the night at Tracy's," I boasted to everyone I saw, and I knew they were envious.

But after an hour or two there, after the games and the snack, homesickness started to creep in. I missed my bed, my other toys; her family ate brown bread, not white; and her house creaked in the wind.

I finally whimpered to Tracy, "I need to go home." Then we trudged sadly to her father, who called my house.

Expecting my mother and sympathy, I felt my heart stop when my father showed up on Tracy's front porch. I can't imagine to this day what he was doing there—he never had anything to do with me. But there he was, big and scary, with tight lips, definitely pissed that I was coming back home. He didn't say a word, didn't hug me or touch me, offered no comforting gesture, just stone silence. I traipsed after him, dragging my sleeping bag and stuffed animals, sobbing and running to keep up, back up the small hill, back through the neighborhood where everyone could see us, as he stormed ahead of me. The kids stopped their games and stared, and I looked away in shame while I fought my growing fear that he would punish me when we got home. But back at our house, he headed into the kitchen and out into the backyard, slamming the door behind him, and, without a word or a fist, he let me know I had failed.

The silent treatment was a common method my father used to diminish me. It went on most of my life. Later, when we moved to Oregon, we lived out in the country, far from my school, and there was no bus. My school was on his way to work, so he reluctantly agreed to let me ride with him. Even though he could have driven the road that passed right by my school, he always chose an alternate route that required me to trudge several blocks. I remember freezing, snowing days when I had books and projects to carry, but he still wouldn't alter his course. I didn't know why. I wanted to ask, but the total silence in the car never gave me an opening. I would get in; he would drive and never say one word to me. A couple of times, I tried to start a conversation, but he ignored me. His tactic was extremely effective—it made me feel as if I had said something dumb, as if I were too inconsequential to merit any of his time, too ignorant to talk to someone as smart as he was. Each day, I arrived at school already feeling tense from the ride into town.

My father also used minor violence and loss of dignity to put down his children. One time, my sister accidentally knocked his bifocals off the dining room table. Later, out in the backyard, where he was watering the lawn by hand with the sprinkler, he waited until she was in a vulnerable position—upside down on our homemade trapeze—then sprayed her with the hose, both punishing and demeaning her at the same time, leaving her with that sense of shame and humiliation that he liked to instill in us. When she told me about it later, I imagined my big sister, my role model and idol, wet and disheveled, whimpering on her bed. The thought made me light-headed, like my brain cells were coming unglued.

Our dinner hour was a prime example of my father's debasement techniques. Every evening, the tension started around five thirty, when he began pacing around, waiting impatiently for his meal, which had to be served at six o'clock on the dot. If dinner wasn't on the table promptly, 6:01 brought about an escalation in his annoyance, along with anxiety on my part, and the strained atmosphere grew and grew with each minute the clock ticked.

By the time we finally sat down, my stomach twisted inside like the two braids down my back. I could feel his irritation as he muttered, "Jee-sus Christ!"

My mother, never sitting down, flitted around the table, serving mashed potatoes and running to get the boiled zucchini and pork chops. My father's requests—more butter, another napkin, "Can you get me a beer?"—would send her scampering off again.

Then he'd say, "I don't want any goddamn babbling at the table about your day. Who has an intelligent subject of conversation for dinner tonight?"

None of us answered, too afraid we wouldn't present an acceptable topic. In my head, I worried that whatever I chose to say would elicit a look of disgust from my father and an implication that I was not only a disappointment but also a halfwit.

One night, my older brother, Mark, finally broke the silence and quavered, "Someone stole my Cub Scout cap off my head today." He lowered his head to hide the tears he was fighting, but I saw them anyway. He loved that hat.

My sister and I started: "Oh no, what happened, how awful, that's terrible, who would do that?"

My father glared at us. "Oh, Christ! Would you all just stop that sniveling? And, Mark, be a man." Without further comment, he reached for his spoon and rapped each of us on the head with it. The sting, plus the added shock, brought tears to my eyes. This happened enough times that when we set the table, we inspected all the dented spoons as evidence of his cruelty.

Of all his behaviors, my father's lack of interest in me was probably the most painful. He never looked at my report card, school projects, clothes, toys, or anything that was important to me as a child. He did not praise me in any way. I can't even remember his ever really looking at me.

One weekend when my mother was gone, I tested whether my father cared about me at all. I stayed out all night, just wandering around town and eventually sleeping at a friend's house. I didn't come home until the next morning, when I traipsed through the front door, wearing my Saturday-night clothes, and passed right by him in the dining room. He was sitting at the table with his shirt off, ready to go play tennis, eating his pregame pancakes, and he didn't even look up from his daily newspaper. I went downstairs to my basement room, sat on my bed, and contemplated how I had just proven that I really was invisible.

I did everything I could to get his attention as I grew up. I took up tennis, his favorite sport; I took advanced math and physics at my country high school, courses that I surmised he would like, since he was an engineer; I got straight A's; I even learned to stand on my head—literally—since he did it every night on the living room rug. None of it impressed him.

There were no other grown male relatives or role models around besides my father—no uncles, one grandpa was dead, the other lived far away, and my parents had few friends over —so I didn't have any examples of acts of kindness from a man. What I knew was that men and boys had the power, girls should do what they said, and they essentially defined us.

Boys came into the picture as romantic objects when I was seven years old, giving me another perspective, and not in a good way. James was my black boyfriend in second grade, when that just wasn't done. I'm sure the people in our 100-percent-white suburban development looked at us askance when he came over to my house, but my mother never said a word about it, so I didn't feel weird back then. But the sad thing is that I had a boyfriend at all at that age, and that my mother encouraged it. She didn't show the same interest in Gary, a boy who was just a friend of mine, as she did in my boyfriends, even though Gary came over to my house often and we played together all the time. In contrast, when a boy I liked romantically showed up, he received lemonade, questions, and more attention. Alone, we would hold hands and kiss each other on the cheek. But the main difference between a friend who was a boy and a boyfriend was that the boyfriend would tell me what to do and make me feel off-base. He was more important than I was, and I would go out of my way to please him.

Such was the case with the bad boy, Bryce, whom I loved in elementary school. At recess, he would demand, "You gotta kiss me" before he would give me the ball, and he'd call after me, "You're a chicken if you don't slap me; I dare you to slap me," when I didn't do it.

I would tail him after school as he walked to his house on the "wrong" side of the tracks. He played to my low sense of self-worth, torturing me with erratic attention and telling me he loved another girl, not me. I ate it up, making friends with her, too, so I could be near him, waiting it out, hoping. He taunted me by giving and taking away his attention, always chasing after another girl, and I totally bought into it. Plus, I put the blame on the other girls, not on Bryce. Today, I find it unconscionable when women blame other women for men's transgressions. I still hear women saying, "She stole my boyfriend"—mad at the girl caught up in the situation, but not the guy.

I wrote about Bryce and the pain and confusion he caused me every day in my diary for six months, plotting about how I could make him call me, like me, pay attention to me, until finally he moved away (thank God).

ONE SUMMER, MY parents and I set out on a trip from Seattle to Montana to visit my father's youngest brother, Jimmy, for a week. I had a thousand questions in my young mind: *Why are we going on this trip? We never go anywhere with Dad. We only had that one trailer trip with him a couple of years ago, and he was mad most of the time. Why are we going to visit Uncle Jimmy? Except for Aunt Mabel, my father hates his eight brothers and sisters because they all used to beat each other up, and his parents got drunk and whipped them. We never see them. But Dad sort of likes Jimmy. I think he helped raise him, and I know he arranged for Jimmy to go to college. He and Uncle Jimmy are the only ones in their family with college degrees, so maybe that's it.*

And, since I'd never gone anywhere with my parents alone, my key question was, *Why am I the only kid going?* I ventured, *Maybe it's because that trailer trip with three kids was too much and he can't tolerate all of us. He wants to have only one kid in the car, and since I'm the smallest, he thought,* I'll take that one. *Or maybe he likes me best?*

Afraid to upset this unexpected favor, I asked no questions and received no explanations. My father picked up my mother and me in Seattle, and my brother and sister, relegated to staying with my grandparents, stood in the driveway and waved good-bye.

We left at night, so that added to the surreal mood of the whole venture. With my pillow, blanket, and stuffed animals, I bounced around in the back, intoxicated by it all—the chosen child, on a trip, at night. I popped up over the front seat, chattering away, but I could see something wasn't right. Tension oozed like sweat out of my father's pores. Before I knew it, my mother turned around, slapped me across the face, and yelled, "Shut up!"

All I remember is complete shock as I fell into the back-seat, whimpering. My mother had never, ever hit me before. But even back then, I could see that it was because of my father. She was afraid of his anger, afraid it would ruin the trip, and so she took his side. He needed total silence, not a child's excited jabbering, so she took care of it. And in the end, it did ruin the trip. We continued down the freeway, quiet and stiff in our seats, as if rigor mortis had set in. Even when we arrived at my uncle's house, I remained quiet and teary-eyed. Normally, in a crowd, I sought out my mother for a quick hug or a hand squeeze, but this time I lost myself in a covey of strange cousins. My parents and I avoided each other in the midst of the other relatives, and then left after only one day, the trip aborted, and drove back to Seattle without a word.

I knew that as long as my father was around, I could get little comfort from my mother. Her inability to defend me made me think, *Mom loves me but won't stand up for me, which must mean that Dad is right—I'm not worth anything.*

Somehow, she couldn't counteract his negativity when she told me in private that I was a good girl. And she never really told me I was smart or talented. My mother's main compliment was that I was "conscientious," so her nickname for me was Connie Ann. It's a fine quality, but not one that gave me any sense of power or strength.

My mother never acted or spoke up in my defense to my father. If he degraded me, she never said, "Harry, stop that right now!" or, "How can you speak to your daughter that way?" or anything else that would have let me know that what he was doing wasn't okay.

It worked the same way later on when men appeared to

condone it if another man insulted me in a corporate meeting. In the room, they wouldn't say anything in my defense—"Hey, that's not fair to say that to her" or, "What do you mean by that?"—even though in my office later, they might tell me, "I can't believe John talked to you like that" or, "He had no business blaming that on you!"

Then I would think, *Where were you when this was happening and you were sitting there watching?* A defense after the fact doesn't work the same as if someone stands up for you in the moment. That's what I needed my mother to do, but she didn't. And I didn't know how to demand that earlier in my work career, when I could have reached out to colleagues for support. A technique I finally learned was to ask someone ahead of a meeting to come to my aid, with examples and that person's endorsement, if a certain topic became controversial. For example, I attended numerous personnel meetings where we decided on high-level promotions. If there was a "preferred candidate" but I thought someone else deserved the position, I'd call a supportive colleague and say, "Could I come by your office and talk to you for a few minutes? When is a good time?"

Seated before his desk in my suit and heels, I'd lay out my reasoning: "I'm going to propose and advocate for Sherry to get the general manager position. Here's why: She nailed the Angola project, she's led her team to accomplish record numbers in the past three years, and she has the highest job rankings of all the candidates."

We'd bounce her qualifications back and forth, and if my colleague were convinced, I'd further ask, "Since you worked with her personally on the Angola project, could you bring up that example in the meeting and give your endorsement?" I'd repeat that several times with fellow managers to make sure we had a plan. There's nothing like another voice, an advocate in the room, to back us up and help us make our case. But we have to speak up and ask for it.

ALL THESE INCIDENTS with my father fed into my later vulnerability to sexual harassment, because my poor self-image and neediness made me an easy target for predators. I felt like a victim time and time again in my childhood, so it's not surprising that I became one later in life. Sexual harassment causes shame within the victim, which was a familiar feeling for me. Combined with my training to be subservient to men, to wait on and cater to them, I was a mess. I clearly saw my parents' roles and, even though I didn't want to be like them, couldn't help reverting to those male dominant–female submissive behaviors as I grew up.

Another result of my troubled relationship with my father was that it made me a dedicated advocate for loving, involved parenting, especially that of a father to his daughter. That connection is all-important in building self-esteem in girls and young women, and it paves the way for their future of healthy interactions with men. I wish I'd had that bond.

In 2017, in an adult Spanish class where I tackled a foreign language at age sixty-five, the teacher's cell phone rang. He clumsily tried to turn it off, then saw it was his grown daughter and answered it in front of the class. In a sweet, cheery voice, he said, "Hi, honey! I'm teaching a class now and can't talk, but I'll call you later, okay?"

She had video-called him, so he turned the phone toward our class and exclaimed, "This is my daughter. Isn't she wonderful?"

We all laughed and smiled, but inside my heart made a

clunk sound and my chest tightened because of envy, yearning, a bottomless cavity in me that still sought a father's approval and love. Images of my father's blankness toward me went through my head, and I remembered how he never, ever said I was pretty or smart or nice or a fast runner or accomplished in any way at all. I had to shake it off, though I marvel now at how a father's kindness toward his daughter still puts a lump in my throat and a glitch in my heart after so many years. I think I'm cured, and then something pops up, I see that the pain is still in there, and I have to work through it.

MY CHILDHOOD ENDED when I was about ten years old, at the start of the 1960s. My father got fired, and we moved from San Luis Obispo to Belmont, in the San Francisco Bay Area. Then he left us.

He came into my room one night, which scared me on its own, because he never did that and, I wasn't sure what he was going to do to me. Just the strong, familiar smell of his sweaty body odor gave me the jitters and a little nausea as he sat near me in my single bed. "Well, Cindy," he said, "your mom and I have been getting on each other's nerves lately, so I'm going to move out and get my own place. I'll be leaving tonight. I only came in to tell you good-bye."

Always hesitant to speak to him, for fear I'd say something that would irritate him or make him think I was stupid, I didn't ask any questions and just said, "Okay."

He left my bedroom, and as I lay there, surrounded by my stuffed animals, I sighed with a delightful and shameful sense of relief.

There was no mention the next day, or any day after that, of my father's departure—no explanation from my mother, no dinner table discussion. He just wasn't there anymore. The four of us pussyfooted around each other for a day or two; then we all relaxed and went on with our lives. My mother didn't cry or flail around in her room; in fact, she seemed almost lighter as she breezed around the house.

We lived a year or so without him, no longer a 1950s nuclear family. I could breathe better and sleep better, and my appetite increased in his absence. There was more laughter in the house, we could talk about whatever we wanted at dinner, and we could flush the toilet after eight in the evening. Ironing his handkerchiefs and shirts, a chore I always resented, was no longer my job. Now that he was absent, I could invite my friends overnight. We could even make a little noise while playing with our Barbie dolls or jumping in the leaves in the backyard, without him there to yell at us.

At the few forced visits we paid to his dreary apartment, I had nothing to say to him as I slouched in a chair across from him at his tiny dining table. My mother always brought one of her homemade pies or a casserole for him and flitted around, pretending we were a normal family. She flirted a little with him and chattered to cover the silence, which served only to irritate my father as he gritted his teeth and forced a smile. Her behavior caused me to worry, *It seems like she still wants to be married to him. Is she trying to get him to come back? I don't want him to live with us again, I like it better without him. Mom, stop it.* We left after only a few minutes each time. I didn't miss him at all.

But then he came back one night and told us we were all moving to Chico, in Northern California, where he had obtained another college professor position. Despite protests and pleas from all of us, we packed up within a couple of weeks and, with my head pressed against the car window, I gasped out shuddered sobs from the backseat the entire three-hour trip as we headed north.

Our duration there lasted only a short time, before my father was dismissed from his job again and announced that we were relocating to Klamath Falls, Oregon. He had total control—there was no family discussion, and I knew my mother, who always seemed as surprised as we felt that we were pulling up stakes, didn't get any input into these decisions to move.

I left childhood and the 1950s and entered adolescence with a hole in me the size of a crater.

LEGAL AND SOCIAL DORMANCY

THE 1950S WERE an awful time for the development of girls and boys in America. Adults of that generation had been raised with even more extreme male–female role definition, and they imposed that on their children. Unfortunately, adult actions affect children for a lifetime. Childhood is a critical span that determines both girls' vulnerability to sexual harassment and boys' tendency to become harassers as grown men.

Many young girls in the 1950s exhibited the same early, natural confidence that I had. For anyone to recognize that girls lost this confidence as they grew up took until the early 1990s, when the American Association of University Women published a report documenting plunging self-esteem in girls as they entered middle school. [1] This report sparked the girl power movement and the numerous publications on girl empowerment that we see today, which is fantastic. [2] But my childhood illustrates the early damage to self-confidence that so many sources, including parents, and especially fathers, cause. Girls of my era did not receive positive messages about our power, achievements, athleticism, or future. We spent scant amounts of time with our fathers, since they all worked and their jobs were primary. Fleeting, awkward moments on the weekends didn't teach most of us to be strong and comfortable around men. We certainly were not educated about how to deal with sexual harassment, since it wasn't even a recognized event.

For boys, the 1950s were a rough time, too. Boys were raised to be macho, not to express emotions. A nice boy was not a strong boy. Perceptiveness about others' feelings was discouraged as "sissy." Boys were taught to believe they were superior to girls, and thereby pressured to be sexual bullies. [3, 4] Many of these boys, like Bryce, grew to torment and disrespect girls at a young age. But there were others, like my poor brother, who happened to be sensitive. I watched him battle my father's scorn and derision. My brother would cry, and my father would scrunch up his face in disgust and shout, "Stop it!"

Thankfully, societal awareness of the need to change this pattern exists today. There is more effort not to ridicule boys if they cry, but they still experience hefty arm twisting to stuff down their emotions, which results in longer-term anger like I saw in my father. The boys of the 1950s had the full-throttle limits of traditional masculinity imposed on them, so they were thwarted in becoming loving, fully functioning parents, partners, and friends. They did not learn that it's unhealthy and unproductive for everyone, and not a sign of strength and power but one of weakness and cruelty.

Working women had a tough go in the 1950s as well. Women experienced some freedom and work opportunities during World War II, when the men left and the women took on their vacated jobs. But they lost those positions when the men returned from war, and many women were forced into domestic roles again as full-time housewives and mothers. Those who did work faced tremendous sexual harassment, since no term for this unchecked male behavior and no legal protection for women existed in the 1950s. When a few women entered the workplace in clerical and manufacturing jobs in the early 1900s, they were subject to physical and verbal harassment from male bosses and workers. For the decades after that, on into the 1950s, this same treatment continued. The only option a woman had if she was sexually harassed was to quit. No one recognized sexual harassment as such, and a woman certainly couldn't complain about it—it was normal, considered natural for men, and perfectly acceptable. [5, 6] A girl's only real job was not to think much of herself, to act inferior to men, and to absorb whatever was dished out to her.

two

KEEP US SILENT

I SPENT THE MAJORITY OF MY FORMATIVE TEEN YEARS IN the 1960s in Klamath Falls, Oregon, a tough, blue-collar, lumber town in the mountains that didn't have much going on. The teenagers were bored and frequently turned to drugs, and not just marijuana, but hard stuff, like heroin. Sexual promiscuity raged, and many of the girls dropped out of high school when they got pregnant. Knife fights after school were not uncommon because of racial tension between whites and the local Klamath Indian tribe.

My brother and sister were both away at college at this point, so I, as the youngest, was the only child at home. I missed my siblings terribly and had no friends in this bleak town where my parents and I had recently moved. I felt pressure at my local school to get involved in drugs, alcohol, and sex, and it seemed like there was no safe place for me. Boys would try to walk me into a dark alley and bear-hug me, slow-dance too close, or creep their hands toward my breasts during a kiss. They'd push for one more drink, try this pill, let's get really stoned. Sometimes I liked the attention, from the right boy, but mostly it was unwanted. I battled them but didn't know how to stop them, so I played along, until often it was too late and I found myself giving in to situations I didn't enjoy at all. I didn't have a clue about what I wanted; I was merely trying to please all males. I once had a date with an Argentinean racehorse heir who attended the local college, and he told me, in his new English, "You have not 'definated' your personality." Boy, was that true—my character was not definite in any way. I felt unsure of myself at every turn.

Longing to get my driver's permit at fifteen, I enrolled in our school driving class. My teacher was a man at least thirty years older than I was—really old to me, more like my father's age. He picked me up in the little blue student driver sedan each Saturday morning, we drove around, I did well, and I was kind of proud of myself.

As he dropped me off after our third lesson, he grinned at me and said, "I can't wait to see you next time."

That didn't sound quite right to me, but I figured maybe he was just friendly—no need to panic—so I gave him a small smile as I exited the car with a wave and said, "Oh, yes, thank you. See you next week."

Craving my permit, I had to finish this driving section of the course with his approval. So I talked myself into staying calm: *Yeah, it's fine. He's only being nice. I feel a little weird, but I'm sure it's okay.*

I hopped into the same blue sedan again the next Saturday morning. This time, my teacher said he had a certificate for me. I opened up the large white envelope he handed me from his driver's seat, tickled that it might be an award I had earned. It looked authentic, but no, it was a certificate for Sexiest Girl in the World. The embossed seal was a woman's leg in a high heel with a garter around the thigh.

The award, made out to me, read, "The abovementioned is hereby authorized to freely participate in any and all activities which come under the general heading of sex."

My heart started to race, but I tee-hee-heed—the nervous

giggle girls gave in those days when men said or did something that made us uncomfortable. I said thanks politely, as I had been taught. Even though a feeling of dread crept into me all through the following week, there I was again the next Saturday, with hope in my heart that I would earn my permit. This was the last lesson—only one more time with him. I knew I could do it. We drove far out into the unpopulated, rural part of town, and he asked me to stop the car. I guessed we were going to practice backing up or turning. But once we were stopped, my teacher leaned over from his place in the passenger seat and began rubbing his hand up and down my leg and gripping the inside of my thigh. My heart thumped, and my throat went dry. I moved away, pretended it hadn't happened, cajoled him into letting me start the car up again, saying, "It's getting late. We should get back. My mom is expecting me," and made it back to town.

When I slouched into my house and past the kitchen, where my mother was rolling out pastry dough for my father's pie, she asked how it had gone and I said, "Fine."

Then I threw myself on my bed in my basement room and twisted around for hours, just defeated. My head swirled: *What is this? What happened in that car? Why is even the smallest attempt to do something like get a driver's license weird, traumatic, and hard?*

Then self-doubt crept in: *Did I do something to encourage this? Why did he choose me?*

Because this man was my teacher and had power over me, I worried, *What if I don't do what he says and wants? I'm dependent on him. Will he not give me my permit if I don't play along? I need him to pass my test. If I don't respond correctly to his sexual advances, will he not sign my course completion?*

Then the self-talk ramped up: *I can't tell anyone, I can't tell anyone, it's horrible, it's my fault, I'm scared he'll hurt me if I tell.*

No one would believe me anyway—he's a grown-up and I'm a kid. Or, worse, he might get angry! And I was still programmed—by my father's anger and my mother's fear of it—never to be around when a man lost his temper.

Further, my mother repeatedly gave me the message that if something happened between a boy and me, somehow it was not his fault, so it must be mine. She had a favorite line—"You know, that poor boy wasn't to blame; it was that woman who talked him into it"—whatever story it was about. My sister and I used to joke later that if we were lying raped and violated in a hospital room, she would rush in and say, "That poor boy, he was just all mixed up. He didn't mean it." She even defended Prince Charles's unfaithfulness to Princess Diana: "Poor Charles! He never wanted to marry her! She trapped him!"

Given all that, I said nothing to her about the driving teacher, knowing that she would say it was my fault. I guess that's where I got the idea that when I was attacked later in life, it happened because of something I did wrong. That said, this was also an era when women were blamed for getting raped—"she must have asked for it"—so I suppose I got some ideas from that as well. Luckily, my driving teacher signed off on my permit, so I didn't have to discuss it with my mother, and I never had to see him again.

MY SISTER WAS attending college back in Chico, California. When my mother said I could go visit her by myself, I discoed around and lip-synced to raucous music every day before the trip. Arriving at her apartment, I swooned when I heard she had arranged for us to go out on a Saturday night with her boyfriend and his two roommates—college men. I couldn't believe my luck.

I dressed up as best I knew how at fifteen and bounced

along behind her to their second-story apartment in an old house, where we were to meet before going out on the town. But after introductions, my sister and her boyfriend disappeared to another apartment across the hall to be alone, and I found myself left with the two roommates who were well into a drinking binge for the night. They knocked back cheap vodka with beer chasers, yelled, and jumped around the room on the furniture while I tried to be a good sport to make them like me, as I'd been taught, smiling and politely trying to laugh. But my stomach clenched as I realized they were over-the-top drunk. Their voices grew louder and wilder, until they were taunting, shouting, "We're going to rape you!"

In my head, I panicked: *Oh my God! What did I do to make them turn on me? I'm trapped in this apartment with them. What should I do? I can't make them mad—who knows what they would do then? They're in charge.*

Eventually, one of the men went to use the bathroom and the other passed out, so I made my move in the few minutes I had. I scrambled out the window, down two stories on a drainpipe wrapped with ivy, and flew out into the night, sweating and shivering at the same time. There was no way to text or call my sister in those days, so I raced as fast as I could, crying, through the dark streets to her apartment complex and hid outside in the juniper bushes until she came home to find me. This became a classic pattern over the years—I was naive, obedient, and full of fairy-tale expectations, while the reality of a situation turned out to be crushing and traumatizing and left me wondering where I had gone wrong.

Girls of my generation had few options but to carry on the marriage-seeking role-modeling of our mothers and grandmothers. We had to get started finding a husband in our teens. If we didn't have a steady boyfriend or engagement locked in by our twenty-first birthdays, we were old maids. I had no clue that this game had different rules for the two sexes. Young men weren't similarly programmed for commitment or settling down.

One evening my friend Ruth and I, on a big night out, drove to Eugene, Oregon, a university town. Our plan was to attend a higher-caliber basketball game than our ho-hum high school events. And this college basketball arena was special—the historic, maple-floored McArthur Court—exotic compared to our local gym. Revved up after the three-point tie-breaking shot, we marched past the fraternity houses to our car parked nearby. Parties were in full swing. Fraternity boys sprawled on the steps outside one house, beckoning us in, "Hey, girls, come to our party. Free beer and music!"

We timidly entered. Before I knew what hit me, a cute boy asked me to dance and I was in heaven. We freestyled and bantered all evening. He asked me to sit on the couch with him and eventually we snuggled and he gave me a deep kiss. My mind went in one direction, *This is it. I've met my knight in shining armor. He'll call me tomorrow, we'll be boyfriend and girlfriend, in love, and eventually we'll marry and have babies.* Then I heard, "Hey Scott! Great party! You gettin' a little before the big day tomorrow?"

"What big day?" I asked.

"Ha! This is Scott's bachelor party. He's getting married in the morning!"

A stabbing pain tore at my heart, but I was sure Scott would break off his engagement before the wedding and become my new beau and eventual fiancé. He got married the next day.

For a short time, I had a boyfriend, Jeff, who was going to college in Portland. Jeff had an art professor who was looking for someone to pose nude for him. Jeff asked me, his sixteen-year-old girlfriend, if I would do it. Trying to accommodate him, as I was conditioned to do with men, I said yes, although internally I screamed the word "no."

When Jeff walked up the front path in the Oregon rain and knocked on the professor's door, I cowered next to him on the covered porch with my head down and my hair in my face. I couldn't make eye contact when the professor opened the door and he was all suave and hip, with a beard, bell-bottoms, and longish hair. His smiling, also hip wife welcomed us into their woodsy, nicely appointed home.

The professor took me to a back room that doubled as a "studio" and asked me to take off all my clothes and wrap myself in a huge piece of see-through plastic while his wife and Jeff drank coffee on the couch in the living room. I didn't want to be there, didn't feel hip, knew this wasn't for me, but I lost my voice and said nothing while I obeyed. The professor raised his camera and told me to act sexy, which I tried to do, even though I didn't really know how. I shut off my brain, hung my hair in my face, closed my eyes, went through silly motions, and got through it. When I look at the photos now, I see my pained expression.

It was all "above board" and for the sake of art, but it felt like exploitation and I hated that professor, exhaling his raspy breath on my face as he closed in, inches away, with his camera in the dark room. To this day, I get angry when I go to art exhibitions and see all the paintings and photographs of female nudes created by famous men, because it all feels to me like a bunch of guys getting off on staring at naked young girls. I recently went to one exhibit like that with my husband, and, much as it upset me, I didn't even know the reason for my anger until I remembered that rainy day in Portland when I felt shamed by art.

However, because of the lack of attention I received during my childhood, I became ever more desperate for it from men. A young, handsome teacher came to town and began working at my high school. He was intelligent and from the "outside world," meaning not Klamath Falls, and I still had few friends and plenty of aching inside. I would stay after school to talk with him, and I loved the way he challenged me intellectually, asked me provocative questions about our class discussions, and assigned me extra work to keep me engaged. I believed he really "saw" me and recognized that I was smart. I wanted to get more of that attention, especially from an authority figure.

I drove to his place one Friday night in my mother's car, wearing a gray dress and jacket I liked, and stopped outside his small house out by the lake. I waited in the dark, my heart pulsing, then knocked on his door with a pretense about a special book, which seemed plausible to me, since I was maintaining good grades in all my classes and I was always asking for additional resources. He came out of his house in shorts and an old T-shirt, with ruffled hair, just hanging out on a Friday night at home, and I hoped that he would invite me in, that we would talk and be close (maybe kiss?), and he might become my boyfriend. I felt a small thrill as we chatted out in his narrow, muddy front yard—but he didn't invite me into his house.

After the book conversation stalled, he told me, "Cindy, you should go home." I sped off with tears running down my cheeks and a new little break in my heart, but for many years I wished I could somehow thank him for having been an exception: *Thank you, thank you, for not taking advantage of my needy, misguided teenage self.* How weird and revealing is that today—to want to thank someone for *not* attacking you?

During my junior year in high school, in 1967, I got my

first job. Newly sixteen, I rushed out and secured my work permit as soon as I was eligible for employment, eager to have my own money, independent of my father, who begrudged every cent he had to spend on me. I worked the night shift in an old barn on a horseradish farm thirty miles out of town. I banged the dirt off the big, gnarly horseradishes as they came in from the field, preparing them for shipment in large dump trucks. The roots came by on a conveyer belt, I'd grab one, shake the hell out of it, and send it on its way down the line. My shift lasted from eight at night until five in the morning, when I sped home to shower off, as I was covered from head to toe in rich black soil, with only my eyes peeking out like a coal miner's. I'd rush off to my class that started at seven, finish up school at three in the afternoon, sprint home, take a quick nap, do my homework, and ready myself for the horseradish shed again.

It was going okay, though my head got all buzzy and my eyes drooped and I barely stayed awake in class, until the one-hour midnight lunch break at work became a problem. A few weeks into the horseradish season, a man on my shift brought in a chess game he had carved with a fancy board and chess pieces. He grasped my arm and pulled me over to the corner of the barn, wanting to show me his handiwork. As I looked closely, I noticed that the pieces were all gruesome, sadistic, and devilish pornography. He badgered me every lunch hour for weeks to come look at each new chess piece he created. I didn't know how to handle it. Since I was reared to be deferential, I believed my job was to compliment him, make him feel like an artist. I hated the sinking tightness in my chest as I tried to avoid him with weak excuses: "I have to get back to work"; "I need to go talk to Janice." But when those weren't effective, I didn't know what to do, so I continued to huddle with him, crouched in the corner of the barn, feeling close to tears.

Luckily, the horseradish season ended eventually and the job was over, so I got away from him. But the experience emphasized how little I knew about how to handle myself and how to react to men's advances and harassment.

Even with all this sexual confusion going on and no academic encouragement from my father (who still didn't think girls should go to college), I continued to do well in high school. I went to three different high schools and was always the "new girl," but I kept up my grades, and my teachers' approval motivated me. However, I eventually found out that my grades didn't mean all would go smoothly.

Since I was the top student in the school my senior year, I got up my nerve to talk to my college counselor about university, despite my father's discouragement. My counselor never brought it up with me, so I had to initiate the conversation. I agonized, *What if I'm wrong and I'm really not smart after all? Is that why my counselor hasn't talked about college with me?*

When I was seated in his cluttered office, he conceded that I might want to try college but said I shouldn't apply to any top-tier schools. "You know," he said, "those schools are too far from home; a girl should stay near her parents and her own town so she can come back if things don't work out. Also, those schools would be really tough to get into and too difficult for you academically." He told me I should just apply to the local college, which was in the bottom rung. I ended up not applying anywhere.

Graduation finally arrived, but it didn't go well. A month before the ceremony, I was selected as valedictorian—the student with the highest grade point average (GPA), in those days a solid 4.0, in my class of more than six hundred seniors.

I puffed up with pride inside, although I tried to show disdain for the whole system externally, still believing it wasn't cool to be smart, especially for a girl.

As valedictorian, I was asked to give a speech at the local Elks club's luncheon. But when I showed up for school the day of the speech, the principal called me into his office because an ad hoc board of men had decided that my skirt was too short. He sent me home crying to change, but when I searched my closet, I realized I didn't have any longer skirts, and in those days, girls couldn't wear pants to school. My mother came to the rescue with a dress of her own, in a brown-and-white silky material that I actually felt kind of pretty in, although I was also mad that I had to look "pretty" in the first place.

A week before graduation, the administration said there was another student, Laura, whose grades were the same as mine, so, without explanation, they decided to revoke my award and bequeath the valedictorian role to her. Laura never asked the teachers challenging questions or raised a controversial issue in class as she sat quietly in the back of the room, her longish skirt tucked tightly over her knees. She wore her blond hair coifed and silky, tied back with a satin ribbon that always matched her dress. The last semester, Laura got an A-minus in one course while I got all A's—so theoretically they should have given the role back to me, but they didn't. I regarded those A's as carved in stone; they were my proof that I was okay, proof that no one could take away from me. But they did. How could this be? I'd put so much into those grades for so long. Injustice ran through my veins, and I saw that for girls, "femininity" and "goodness" superseded academic ability.

At graduation (wearing leather sandals under my robe, in lieu of beige pumps), I still gave a speech, as the second-place salutatorian, but at the last minute I changed it from the approved speech I'd submitted to the administration. Instead, I said what I wanted: "Your children are not your children," I quoted from Kahlil Gibran in a rebellious tone, while the audience tittered and parents and teachers shook their heads.

My mother, seated up in the bleachers in the gym, said she was embarrassed—especially later, when the host of the local radio talk show, whom everyone listened to in our small town, derided me as "disrespectful" and "radical." Callers accused me of pitting children against their parents and inciting wanderlust in teens. Of course, I wanted my mother to be proud because I had spoken up and expressed myself. And more than anything, I wanted my father, a bit of a rebel himself, to approve. He wasn't doing anything the night of graduation but still didn't come, commenting only, "Cindy, I don't like ceremonies. I find them boring and irritating."

That haunted me for years—his discounting of me, of my one accomplishment as a smart, good student. I had no proof that I was pretty or talented or nice or anything else; this was it—my good grades and this honor were all I had—and it meant nothing to him. This became a topic for many therapy sessions later in life.

At the final hour of the summer after graduation, when job prospects looked bleak for someone with only a high school degree, I decided to apply to one school: Reed College in Portland, Oregon. My main reason, aside from the pitiful job opportunities for me locally, was that my boyfriend, Jeff, the one from the naked art incident, lived in Portland. This was a developing pattern with me—making life decisions based on proximity to prospective men. I had been taught that a girl needed a man, that they were all-knowing and that I shouldn't trust my own instincts but should follow what a man said or did.

When my acceptance letter arrived with a scholarship included, I clutched it to my chest as if I were embracing a long-lost friend. Then I recalled how discouraging my high school counselor had been, and I thought, *That man had no idea what was best for me. I ignored his advice, made my own decision to apply to Reed in spite of him, and look what happened.* The thing about authority figures is that, no matter how powerful they may seem or what professional distinction they have, they don't always know what's best for you better than *you yourself* do.

My parents and I drove off in September 1969 to Reed—my father in his old station wagon and my mother and I in her little white Rambler. I wasn't sure why we had two vehicles, but I relaxed and slept, glad not to have Dad in the car as I rode shotgun.

When we arrived at ivy-covered Reed College, where all the deciduous trees were gold for the fall, my heartbeat quickened a little as I spotted the other students and parents and felt the excitement of this special launch day. Then, as I bounded out of the car, my father said to me, "Well, I'll be driving back to Klamath Falls, and your mother is going to Eugene."

"What? What's going on?"

"Your mom has arranged for an apartment in Eugene and is moving there today. Oh, and we're getting a divorce."

It was evident to me, from the relaxed way in which my father broke the news, that the divorce was his idea. My mother barely said a word, just helped me quickly dump my suitcase and boxes in my dorm room. The day was a bust for me (and for her, too, I'm sure). I thought, *I'm responsible for my father's misery. I was the obstacle to his getting what he wanted—his freedom—and he just waited it out until the final minute, when I was out of there. The crime I committed was being the last child to leave home.*

Other students had their parents hanging around and helping them settle in, but mine hit the road after about thirty minutes. They started up their car engines, and I stood in my college dorm parking lot and watched them pull away in opposite directions.

My father had his college professor job, the house, his friends, his town of Klamath Falls. My mother was the one who had to leave, find a job, make new friends, start from scratch, and live in low-income housing while my father kept the nice house on the lake. Somehow, following the divorce, she had no money and he had plenty. I couldn't fathom how that had happened. I wondered, *In a divorce, aren't you supposed to split the money equally? And doesn't the abandoned one get more of the money as some kind of recompense?* Interestingly, I blamed my mother at the time: *Why didn't she stand up for herself? Why did she let him have the money and the house and his life untouched? Why did she live poor and have to work as a low-paid secretary, her first job in thirty years, after he left?*

I remember one lonely Christmas in her one-bedroom, low-rent apartment when I was in college, and the only kid home. She had burned the string beans, and it was enough to make her crack. She threw the saucepan across the kitchen, screaming, "Everything is so unfair! I'm alone. Not having a man is the worst thing that can happen to a woman. I'm trapped. A woman can't go anywhere without a man, and I don't have one."

I stood stock-still and stared at her. We didn't emote like this in my family. I wanted to hug her and punch her at the same time. Today, I look at the incident through the lens of her own self-esteem—if I thought mine was low, just imagine what her experiences were in her generation. She never believed she was worth much at all, so she couldn't instill a sense of self-worth in her children or stand up for herself or any of her kids. But at the time, I felt only waves of anger and disgust. I hated seeing her weakness. I loved her, but my vow never to be anything like her was in full flower by then.

Shortly after I started college, on the brink of the 1970s, Jeff and I broke up. I was a little older now, a college girl. I'd been burned one too many times, I was sick of my social conditioning, and I didn't want to be bossed around by a boy or beholden to his wishes. *Now*, I thought, *I will have my own money and my own life, and no man is ever going to get the better of me.* I had no idea how hard it was going to be to actualize that declaration.

SEEDS OF LEGAL AND SOCIAL CHANGE

MY SOCIAL BELIEFS in the 1960s were affected by the attitudes of the time about female roles in school, as well as in the workplace. Girls were not encouraged in school, and I was the lone girl in my physics class—the only advanced science class my high school offered. Girls were seen as "helpers"—a concept that, sadly, hasn't completely changed yet. Girls continue to lack confidence and are conditioned to avoid leadership. A 2017 study of more than ten thousand girls in the United States revealed that one in three girls ages ten to seventeen are "afraid to be a leader for fear of others thinking she is bossy." [1] And 46 percent believe that "speaking their mind or disagreeing with others will keep people from liking them." Researchers found in the same study that the percentage of girls who describe themselves as confident declines from 86 percent at age ten to 60 percent at age twelve. By high school, 46 percent of girls with a GPA over 4.0 do not think they are smart enough for their dream career. In other current survey work, it was noted that six-year-old girls "are less likely than boys to believe that members of their gender are 'really, really smart.' Also at age six, girls begin to avoid activities said to be for children who are 'really, really smart.'" [2]

Just as I had signed on for my first job as a farmworker in the 1960s, more women were entering the workplace at this time. At the start of the decade, 38 percent of women over sixteen years old participated in the workforce, while in 1970, just ten years later, female participation was 43 percent, a sizable jump. [3] My fledging efforts at independence were difficult, however, because in the 1960s there were no laws to protect women against sexual harassment. One of my friends told me that her father-in-law often said, "I loved the workplace in the sixties. We could call women 'broads,' slap their asses, pour ourselves a scotch at ten in the morning, and light up in the office. Those were the good old days."

Sexual harassment still did not have a name, but its visibility was increasing, since more women were present in offices and work facilities. That decade saw the institution of the 1964 Civil Rights Act and Title VII, which prohibited discrimination in employment because of sex, but did not address sexual harassment—what to do about it or that it even existed. It took years for courts and lawmakers to create laws defining the sex component of the Civil Rights Act. No cases came to court until over a decade later, and the Supreme Court didn't hear a sexual harassment case until 1986. [4] The National Organization for Women (NOW) was formed in 1966, which gave us girls an inkling that we might be stronger than we realized. I read about it and was inspired, but it was far away from me, and there certainly was not a NOW chapter in Klamath Falls.

My brain was a big, messy jumble about men and sex during this time, and no wonder—there were mixed messages everywhere in the '60s. There was still the old rule that women needed to be virgins at all costs when we got married—and we knew getting abused or raped would count against us and was mostly "our fault." It was unacceptable if we didn't land a man. A bad boyfriend was better than no boyfriend. We had to have one. But we were also supposed to be "free," as the hippie movement told us. We dreamed we might get jobs, unlike our mothers, but the jobs couldn't challenge men. They would have to be acceptable "support" roles, like nurses and secretaries.

Helen Gurley Brown's 1962 book, *Sex and the Single Girl*, compounded the confusing contradiction about a woman's purpose in the workplace. Her advice to us: "Career girls are sexy. . . . A career is the greatest preparation for marriage. You are better organized, better able to cope with checkbooks, investments, insurance premiums, tradesmen, dinner parties and the mixing of a really dry manhattan. You know how to please men." [5]

Brown went on, "What you do from nine to five has everything to do with men anyhow. A job is one way of getting *to* them. It also provides the money with which to dress for them and dress up your apartment for them. . . . Most importantly, a job gives a single woman something to *be*. A married woman already *is* something."

We didn't know what to think, how to behave in the workplace, or why we were there in the first place.

It was inconceivable in the 1960s that a woman would put her career first. She might have a job, but certainly not a *career*. If a woman had a job, it was part-time and flexible so she could attend to her husband and children at any moment. Even Katharine Graham, elected president of the *Washington Post* in 1963 and one of the few high-level professional women in the 1960s, said her insecurity in the job arose from the fact that women had been "brought up to believe that our roles were to be wives and mothers, educated to think that we were put on [E]arth to make men happy and comfortable and to do the same for our children." [6]

Though men in the new millennium have recognized and struggled with work–life balance more frequently, for most of my working life, it remained an exclusively female issue. A 2014 study of four thousand executives confirmed that the tension between work and family is still viewed as primarily a women's problem. [7] Throughout my career, and even now, concerned women ask me, "How did you do it all? How did you have three children and rise up as an executive? Do you cook dinner for your family?"

Typically, I answer these questions by telling women, "Don't try to do it alone. Get help—from parents, friends, relatives, paid workers, whoever. Make friends with nonworking mothers—they're a godsend—but be sure to offer them something in return, like a Saturday-night sleepover if they picked up your child after daycare because you had a critical meeting that went until eight o'clock. And if you get married, be sure you marry a liberated person who isn't threatened by your work and who will do an equal share of the housework and kid work—and all of it if you're on a business trip. Marry a partner."

Men in the 1960s were not expected to be fathers or partners—they worked and provided. They never got asked, and still rarely do today, about their work–life balance.

But the 1970s were coming, and some things, at least for women, did start to change.

PART II

1970s–1980s

three

KEEP US DOWN

EVEN THOUGH TODAY I DON'T BELIEVE IN VICTIMHOOD, I was a victim in many ways in the '70s—of the times and the attitudes, of the sexist messages I received as a girl, and, as a consequence of those, of my own insecurities. My life veered up and then down again, one boot ahead, then a slip back, like hiking a muddy slope, as I tried to make my way.

I gave up my childhood nickname, Cindy, in favor of my birth name, Lucinda—a small thing but a big deal to me. I didn't want to be Cindy anymore. That name was cute and girlie—like some team's B-squad cheerleader, and there seemed to be a lot of teenage girls' horses named Cindy—and that wasn't how I wanted to be viewed. I longed for a gender-neutral name like Lee, so no one could tell ahead of time if I was male or female; I thought it could give me an edge if people suspected I was a man. But Lucinda was what I had to work with, so I went with that.

College itself progressed reasonably well, and I found some level of emotional and intellectual comfort there, since Reed attracted a scholarly, open-minded bunch. As one student said, "If you didn't fit in during high school, there's a good possibility you'll fit in at Reed." Being "smart" was cool. The focus was on learning, not on grades, so that helped ease my obsession with them to prove myself worthy. Teachers filed marks with the registrar, but we did not receive grade reports. They returned our papers with lengthy comments but no grade. There was no honor roll or valedictorian. I didn't have to erase my assignments or do my homework in secret or play dumb in attempts to be liked. Reed was a liberal, "hippie" school, but challenging academically, which suited me. I enjoyed the freedom of expression it allowed both in and outside the classroom.

However, I had no women teachers. There was one female biology teacher whom I saw from a distance and was curious about, but I didn't get to know her. At first I thought she was a lab assistant, but I later found out she was indeed a professor. That fascinated and puzzled me. She wasn't married, of course, since most professional women were single in those days. All my professors and the scientists who wrote and starred in my textbooks were men, so that slowed my aspirations. I continued getting high appraisals from my instructors but still pondered, *I hope I'm pleasing my teacher. I wonder if he notices me. I hope he likes me. Does he think I'm intelligent?*

Reed's equal balance of genders—roughly 50 percent of the student body was female—planted a seed of possibility in my mind. I decided to major in science—in biology, specifically. I had always loved the natural world and the outdoors. When I was a child, my mother used to tell me the names of all the plants growing in our garden while I followed her around our yard. I pictured myself as a national park ranger, out on my beat, keeping the forest safe and the animals and trees healthy. Biology was a man's major, but at Reed, with its enlightened views, no one discouraged me.

In fact, Dr. Bert Brehm, a biology teacher, actually encouraged me and never tried anything untoward with me. His passion for plants and the zeal he exuded cast a science spell over me. Dr. Brehm took our class out on amazing field trips all over the beautiful state of Oregon. We went for hikes, in awe of every natural resource we saw, inspired by his energy and enthusiasm, while he ran around with his hand lens glued to his eye and a quirky field hat pulled tightly over his ears. He invited me to do a special algae project in his laboratory, even though I was only a freshman, and I was in heaven. First and foremost, I still craved male attention—so getting his approval and notice was the most important thing to me. But a close second was the science itself. I grew colonies of green, spherical Volvox algae, the most exquisite creatures I'd ever seen, and I exalted in discovering ways to help them to survive and flourish.

But then, suddenly, my father would pop back into the picture and I'd backslide. Early in my freshman year in 1970, I had my wisdom teeth pulled and was recovering at my mother's affordable housing unit, which she qualified for in Eugene because of her meager income. My father was visiting her—he came to see her occasionally, and they slept together and presumably had sex. I always cringed about her giving herself to him like that, but when I mentioned it, she said, "You have no idea how hard it is for me without a man." Too bad she didn't think it was better for her without a man like my father.

Soon after I got home from the dentist, Dad asked me to play tennis with him. He never, never asked me to do anything with him, so I thought, *Oh, how flattering. He thinks I'm good enough to play tennis with him. I learned to play tennis to be like him, but he's never played with me. Maybe this is my big break to impress him. Then he'll respect me for my athletic ability and he'll give me more attention in the future. We can talk about tennis!*

My mother said, "Harry, she can't play—she just had surgery."

But he insisted, "Aw, she can do it. She's tough. Right, Cindy?"

I winced but hobbled out the door to the courts. Every time he hit the ball to me, its jarring contact with my racket sent a beam of pain all the way up my arm, into my face and my mouth. But I clenched my teeth, thinking, *I'm tough. I deserve this attention. I can't blow it.*

After I hit a few balls long, he stopped in disgust and said, "Let's go. You shouldn't play tennis with anyone until you're good enough."

We drove home in silence, my hopes for his approval dashed. In the quiet front seat of the car, I wondered, *Did I just fail some kind of test? Did he specifically wait until I had a handicap to ask me to play tennis with him? Was he trying to humiliate me? It felt like a form of taunting, an opportunity to put me down in order to build himself up.* This train of thought further reinforced my already self-deprecating and low opinion of myself.

The small things ratcheted up over time. The process was slow, but the result was that I was forever vulnerable to hope, approval, or anything that might bring me some attention or acknowledgment that I existed. Since I didn't know the term "sexual harassment" then, it wasn't until much later that I realized my dad's behavior on the tennis court had smacked of sexual harassment and thought, *Can a girl be sexually harassed by her own father? Is that what he was doing?*

THE SUMMERS DIDN'T help my self-confidence, either. Sexual harassment reared its ugly head again as I entered the working world to support myself between school years.

The summer of 1970, after my freshman year, as was my

pattern, I followed a boyfriend who was working in western Massachusetts that season. I moved to Boston, close enough to see him some weekends, and found work as a maid at a rundown Ramada Inn outside the city. It was a long, hot ride to the motel from my shared apartment in Cambridge on the used bike I had purchased for $10. But I grinned and pedaled enthusiastically, through miles of smelly traffic, in Boston's summer heat and humidity, in celebration of the fact that I had landed a job. The pay wasn't great, but I was told I could make an extra $1 each time I cleaned up vomit.

The first day I showed up, I was one of four young women who were new motel maids. We were told to report to the supervisor's office. We lined up in front of his wooden desk, standing, and he told us he hadn't picked out our uniforms yet and wanted us to model some possibilities for him.

He showed us to a closet and told us, "Put on the first outfit." It was a tight, black, very short number, but we changed and pranced out to show him.

"Now, turn around and bend down to see if the uniform will work for scrubbing bathtubs and making beds. No, that one won't work. Try another." So we did, about four different uniforms, all tight, all sexy, and all requiring demonstration for ease of turning, bending, kneeling, and stretching.

None of the new maids said a thing. We glanced away, unable even to make eye contact with one another. Even though my stomach lurched during the modeling session, I just didn't trust my own instincts, couldn't go against what I had been taught—to obey, to please, and to smile.

I remember liking one of the uniforms, thinking I looked cute in it, and hoping he would pick that one. Little did I know, the whole exercise was nothing more than an exploitation tactic for the boss's sexual pleasure. The next day, they handed us our uniforms, and mine was a size D, piss-yellow, below-the-knee number that fit me like a grocery sack.

I learned to make a mean bed in record time, but also, more important, I learned something from the older, immigrant maids, who told me, "You shouldn't get on your knees to scour a tub, because you shouldn't get on your knees for anyone, ever."

I had never heard that kind of stand-up-for-yourself message before, as small as that was.

I patted myself on the back when I got another job to supplement my minimal maid income, this time at a Roy Rogers roast beef restaurant ("Is that Trigger?" was the classic customer line, said while pointing at the hamburgers). Speaking of uniforms, I liked that one. In my red-checkered, cap-sleeved blouse, black culottes, string tie, and red cowboy hat, I thought I looked quite sharp. But so did the manager, Chris, who proceeded to squeeze the butts and the hips of me and all the other women who worked there, threatening us with dismissal if we complained: "Just enjoy it if you want to keep working here."

Of course, I disliked it immensely but surmised I couldn't do anything about it. But there were other girls there who knew they could, and they did. They were from Wellesley, Smith, and Brown and apparently had better self-esteem and confidence than I did, because they organized a strike against Chris. I joined in immediately. How empowering! We made placards—"Down with Sexism!" and "Don't Touch Our Bodies"—and marched outside the restaurant.

Some of the male workers joined in, too, which made a big impression on me. There were in fact supportive and kind men in the world who didn't think sexual harassment was right— and who were willing to speak out and take a stand about it.

We actually got Chris fired. I cheered inside to the point of bursting. I didn't know you could say anything about sexual harassment out in public, out in the world. And it was amazing that we got results and nothing bad happened. None of the victims was blackballed or terminated. Only the harasser was punished, as it should be. A tiny awakening made me think, *There might be another way*, but it couldn't immediately overpower years of self-demotion and doubt.

One of the girls at the restaurant introduced me to her uncle Louie, a well-known attorney at Guterman, Horvitz, Rubin, Rudman, and Katz in downtown Boston. He came in now and then for coffee and to visit his niece, and I got to know him a bit. One day, he was lounging in one of the booths and asked me to sit down with him. He asked me about my current employment and my future, and when he heard about my two jobs, he said, "You can do better than working as a motel maid and waitress. Come work for me! I'll pay you twice what you're making now in both jobs."

His confidence in me was just what I needed. *Maybe I am selling myself short*, I thought, and I quit the Ramada and Roy Rogers and headed for the law firm. I treasured my new, prized messenger position, in which I took taxis all over Boston, delivering legal packages to clients in the days before faxes and email. In my spare time, I conducted research in the law library for the other lawyers. A respectable job! I loved the work, and all summer my heart was warm with gratitude for the opportunity and the fact that no one harassed me. The six names of the decent partners in that firm still roll right off my tongue today.

At lunchtime, I explored downtown Boston. When I passed by construction sites (which were on every corner that summer), in direct contrast with the nonsexual atmosphere in the law office, men whistled and yelled comments like, "Hey, baby! Nice tits! Wanna screw?"

I smiled and waved in a shy way, uncomfortably enjoying the attention and what I had been taught to take as compliments. Then, one day, I passed another construction site, but none of the workers said anything to me. I thought, *What's going on? Am I undesirable? Am I ugly?* I deduced that if men noticed me, no matter what they said, that was good and reinforced that I was attractive. It was a compliment. If attention was withheld, it meant I was no good, not cute enough for anyone to notice. How fucked up is that? I didn't know until later in my career that sexual harassment is not an expression of sexual desire, but rather an exercise of power.

One evening I had to work a little late, so I rode my bicycle from the city back home to Cambridge in the dim light. As I was pushing my old, one-speed bike across Harvard Square, a cute medical student stopped to talk to me, and we quickly got fired up discoursing about science.

He said, "I have really interesting research going on in the medical school laboratories. Would you like to see the lab?"

Harvard! The lab! A chance to see high-level science in action! I strode with him over to the medical building. With his own keys, he opened up the large glass doors, since they were locked after-hours. But when we got inside and moved down the hall, he started grabbing and pawing me, and I realized this was not about science. I blasted out of the building, jumped on my bike, and pedaled frantically all the way home, in a fearful sweat.

I beat myself up for years over that one. I concluded that the incident was my fault because I was so ignorant. But did being naive and stupid give a man the right to trick me and attack me?

⌒

BACK AT COLLEGE in 1971, when I was nineteen, my friend Hazel and I rented an old, one-bedroom, barely furnished apartment over a bar. It was inexpensive but a fair distance away from the Reed College campus, so I sometimes hitchhiked to school if I was running late. On one day like this, a nice-looking, middle-aged man picked me up and said he'd drive me all the way to school. *Great!* I thought, as I clambered into his sports car.

As we barreled along, I noticed he had turned off in the wrong direction. When I shifted over in my seat to tell him this wasn't the right way, I saw that he had his erect, blue-veined penis out in his hand. He stroked it and grinned at me.

With a massive lump in my throat, I asked, "Could you please let me out at the next corner?"

But he said, "No, sweet thing."

He kept driving and driving while he masturbated. Finally, at a stoplight, I bolted out of the car and raced away, my books clasped to my chest. Without looking back, I sprinted for blocks, until I gasped for breath and rushed behind a convenience store to hide. He didn't follow me, but now I was miles from school, emotionally undone, and I missed my class. Just a simple thing like trying to go to school on an average morning had turned into a nasty nightmare. It didn't occur to me I should stop hitchhiking—everyone did it, and I had to get to campus. There was no other way—no bus or Uber, and I couldn't afford a taxi—so I waited for a woman to offer me a ride and hitchhiked back to Reed.

But after that incident, I wondered, *Was I asking for it by hitchhiking? Is hitchhiking a sign you're a prostitute? It was my fault that happened, right? Why am I having these incidents? Was my skirt too short? Did I deserve it?*

I still struggled with it all—the guilt, the self-blame, the powerlessness. During my sophomore year, I traipsed nightly past the two gingko trees at the entrance and into the central reading room of Reed's Tudor-Gothic-style library. I pored over my textbooks until the morning light peeked in the windows, since the library stayed open twenty-four hours, kept company by two lovers who routinely slept there overnight. But I found myself distracted from my science pursuits and instead scrounged the stacks for world maps and books about international locales, my head filled with dreams of foreign adventures. *I'm young and free*, I thought. *I should be out in the world, not plopped in a school chair, book-learning about life. I want to* live *life*. Sitting in a classroom, being babysat by professors, paled in comparison with visions I had of vagabonding around the world as a famous biologist in exotic jungles. But I couldn't figure out how to make that happen with my limited qualifications, so I conjured up the second-best idea: Inspired by airline ads claiming that I could "see the world," I decided I would drop out of school and become a flight attendant—known then as a stewardess. I qualified: nineteen years old (the minimum age), tall (but not too tall; at five foot seven, I was under the five-nine cutoff), thin (but not too skinny; I just made it past the lowest weight level of 105 pounds), female, and single. Shamefully, those were the actual job criteria back then, and I knew you could get fired if you gained weight and you'd have to retire at thirty-two. I didn't think about the obvious weirdness and sexism behind those standards until two questions on the application gave me pause.

"Are you now or have you ever been a member of the Communist Party?" I hadn't, but the question seemed odd to me. Even though my politics were minimal because I couldn't vote yet, I had campaigned for George McGovern, the liberal, antiwar candidate for president, and didn't think it was any of the airline's business anyway.

Then the final question pulled me up short: "Do you agree to accept any and all makeover suggestions and alterations to your hair, makeup, and clothes? If you wear eyeglasses, you are not eligible."

That put a stop to the whole idea. Cutting my hair and wearing a big, puffy 'do were out of the question, and yes, I wore eyeglasses, still haunted by the age-old taunt "Men don't make passes at girls who wear glasses." I dropped my pen and tossed the application in the wastebasket. I now know that at that time, airline stewards and stewardesses were working to change flight attendants from sex symbols into actual career employees, but they weren't there yet. I decided to keep pursuing science, which seemed less sexist. But it all turned out to be relative.

THERE WERE OTHER jobs in those summers between college semesters. When I turned twenty, I worked at a girls' summer camp in Maine run by two brothers, Roger and Chuck, who hired only women. We counselors mooned around in the staff cabin, singing to Carol King's *Tapestry* album ("So Far Away"), dreaming of boys left behind. Roger and Chuck were the only men in this isolated enclave in the mountains by lovely little Trout Lake, where we canoed and swam. I taught tennis and botany, both of which I loved, and took care of a cabin full of lively ten-year-olds.

Roger ruled with an iron fist. There were dozens of regulations we had to follow to the letter or else get "talked to." I bristled at the thought.

Roger also fancied himself a god. He dressed all in white, and on Sundays, in a command performance at dawn, he would gather up his female flock, lead us up the mountain, and preach to us while the sun rose. As he read his own poems, he professed he had a heart full of love.

One day he called me into his office, and while I quivered in front of him in his side chair, he said, "Most women's voices are soft and beautiful. But you have the worst singing voice of any female I've ever heard. It's deep and off-key. When we sing in the cafeteria before each meal, I forbid you ever to sing again. You're damaging the children's ears and their psyches."

Shades of my father and the tennis game. So, the rest of the summer, I sat there with my mouth clamped shut and my face red, suppressing tears, while the little girls asked, "Why aren't you singing? Sing with us, please!"

Even though I couldn't apply it to myself, I told them, "I've been asked not to, so I can't. But don't you ever let someone tell you not to sing. You sing all you want whenever you want. Even if you're not good at something or can't do it perfectly, you should still try and not give up, no matter what anybody says. The only way to get better is to press ahead with it."

I didn't sing again in public until almost fifty years later, when my musical and supportive nephew assured me I wasn't tone deaf. Even though I'd gone against my high school counselor's advice, I hadn't yet learned not to internalize and obey everything authority figures told me.

THE SUMMER I turned twenty-one, I started a clam cannery on Mummy Island, near Cordova, Alaska, with four friends. A state full of men but few women resulted in constant sexual comments, whistling, and staring wherever I went. On Mummy Island, I had the company of another woman besides me, and the three men our age saw us as fellow clamdiggers. But after we excavated enough Alaskan razor clams from a week or so of sunrise clamming and several days of canning in our rundown shed, we'd head into the town of Cordova in our small fishing boat to try to sell them, and I couldn't go two feet along the sidewalk without hearing sexual comments from strangers.

It reminded me of the Boston construction-site episodes. Old social messages that trained me to take these remarks as compliments reared up in my head. But by this time, I was sick of it. And mad. Though I still couldn't take off my muzzle and voice it out loud, I glowered at them, hoping they caught my message: *I'm nothing but a sex object to you. I can't even live my life off the island, because of your incessant heckling and harassment. I'm a businesswoman—show some respect! This is exhausting. Leave me alone, you disgusting creeps!*

BACK AT REED for my junior year, I began to worry about my prospects. When I told people I went to Reed College, they would often say, "That's one of those ivory-tower, liberal-arts schools. How are you ever going to get a job with a degree from there?" That rankled in my mind, so I applied to the University of California right at the end of the second semester. This college had a plant biology program emphasizing agriculture, rather than pure botany like I had been studying at Reed, and I figured I would be more employable with that degree. Making my own money so I would never have to rely on a man was a high priority for me, so I imagined future, lucrative work.

Awarded a scholarship in 1972 for those good grades I'd

earned at Reed, I basked in the recognition as I left Oregon to finish my senior year in California.

At first, I waitressed nights to supplement my scholarship. I had recently turned twenty-one and found a job serving cocktails, desirable because of the tips, at a place called Mr. Don's Restaurant. The job went well, but it was hard work—carrying heavy trays of drinks in heels and the required short skirt. I claimed fame for remembering each customer's order, even at a big table, without writing it down.

Shortly after I started working there, Mr. Don, the owner, asked me out.

I said, "No, thank you. I don't date people from work," turning him down carefully and trying to manage his ego so he wouldn't take it personally.

Even though I wouldn't have dated him in a million years —he was twice my age; married, with four children; and overweight, with a greasy, bulbous face, poochy lips, and slick, matted hair—I had been taught to preserve a man's psyche at all costs. And, of course, I feared for my job.

Mr. Don glared at me, augmenting my angst, and said, "We'll see about that."

After I'd been working there for a couple of weeks, the slightly older, blond hostess asked me if I wanted to go out with a few of the other workers after we closed. As the new girl, I thought, *Oh! How flattering! They want to befriend me*, and I smiled a big yes to her.

When we closed at two in the morning, she said, "Let's go out back; the others are waiting in their cars for us."

I followed her out, and she told me to get in the backseat of a big, fancy black Buick that didn't look like something a waiter or cook would own. When I slipped in, I saw Mr. Don sprawled on the seat, alone.

I hesitated and asked, "Where are the others? What's going on?" But by then it was too late—Mr. Don pulled me in, and we took off.

I recognized the driver, Arnie, the owner of Arnie's Restaurant, an old, married Italian man and friend of Mr. Don's. As Arnie and the blond hostess cuddled up to each other in the front seat, I guessed they were having an affair, thinking, *Oh, no. Is this a double date?*

A few miles from the restaurant, Mr. Don grabbed me, kissed me, touched my breasts, and put his hand up my waitress skirt. He persisted, all over me, as we scuffled. I held my arms straight out to keep some distance, but he crushed me to him.

"Be a sport," he said, but I hunched in the corner of the backseat and wouldn't "cooperate."

He sighed in disgust, pouted, then growled, "Let's go back."

They dumped me in the deserted alley by the restaurant at three o'clock in the morning and screeched away in the Buick. I slumped against the alley wall, shaking from the onslaught, *My boss just assaulted me as part of a sleazy ambush. What's going to happen with my job? And I had looked up to that older hostess; I thought she wanted to be my friend. I wanted to meet other colleagues and be part of the team, but it was just a setup for Mr. Don. I've been pimped out.*

I shuffled home alone in the dark, alternately crying and swearing. I wept on and off most of the night, tossing around in my tangled sheets. But I got up the next day, biked to my science classes, and rode to my shift at work that evening. When I arrived, my name was not on the schedule.

Mr. Don stood at the bar, wiping shot glasses. I said to him, "Excuse me, I'm supposed to work tonight, but my name isn't on the list," and he turned his back on me.

I thought he didn't hear me, so I said it again and then

realized he was purposely cold-shouldering me. I didn't know what to do, so I crawled away. With the scrap of strength I mustered up after considerable anguish, I biked back later to confront him again, and this time he just said, "You don't work here anymore."

I went home and cried on my mattress on the bedroom floor at the injustice of it all. *I'm so humiliated. I can't believe the way the hostess and her boyfriend and Mr. Don played me. I need this job to live, and now I've been molested and fired.*

The next day, I scanned lawyers in the Yellow Pages and found one I could ride my bike to, then called and asked for an appointment. On the phone, I told him how I had lost my job because I wouldn't have sex with my boss, who had attacked me.

He said, "Now, now, you should just forget it. Mr. Don is an important man in this town, and he will ruin your reputation if you bring this up. It will be worse for you if you say anything."

When I slammed down the phone after that conversation, I was convinced that the whole world was against me. Of course, there were no female lawyers I could call in the early 1970s, so it had to be a man. And there were no employment lawyers who specialized in sexual discrimination and harassment, like there are today. I'm sure that lawyer had no training in this area, and I knew he didn't completely believe me anyway. I fantasize now about what would have transpired if I could have talked to a woman attorney and she had said, "Yeah! Let's take it to the Supreme Court!" If she had been even the tiniest bit supportive, I would have gone for it. As it was, when this male lawyer told me no, I just backed down, boiling inside. *I hate him. How can he say there's nothing I can do about this? Nothing? Are we women just helpless? Do we have no choice but to take it and shut up?*

This "quid pro quo" was a normal, daily experience for many of my women friends. The reality for us: If you want to keep your job, you need to put out. And we didn't know what to do about it. We were still brainwashed to believe that men just couldn't help it, that their sex drive was uncontrollable, and that when they saw a pretty young lady, well, there was nothing they could do but act out. But the truth is, most harassers know exactly what they're doing. They gain a sense of control by making others feel as if they have no control. They go after the vulnerable person and figure out how to humiliate her. It's a classic form of bullying.

I remember thinking at the time, *Why did he do this? Mr. Don has everything. He owns the best restaurant in town, he has a family and respect in the community. If I had what he has, I would be so happy and grateful and never mess it up.* All I could imagine then was that he was afraid of getting old. Another waitress had joked about his sagging skin and flaccid cheeks beneath a graying beard. He might have been handsome, maybe even a lady's man, in his youth with formerly jet-black hair and olive skin. Perhaps he cut a slim figure before middle age bloated his belly. Maybe he thought a young girl would make him feel like that desirable young man again.

But today, I can't make excuses for him anymore. There are plenty of older women around who I'm sure wish they were young again and I don't see them attacking young boys. My guess is that he, and other men like him, are more like bad dogs that scratch and bite greedily for self-gratification, never trained properly to behave. I can just see him as a child beaten for his misdeeds and seething inside for revenge. I picture his parents and coaches screaming at him from the football field sidelines, "Go get that kid! Knock him down! Don't be a sissy! You're bigger than him." And then his father and other men telling him, "Sow your wild oats, get some while you can," so that he grew up undisciplined, selfish and aggressive, a tyrant towards anyone smaller or lower in the power chain.

ALL MY FEMALE friends in the 1970s knew that medical professionals exploited their authority over women patients. We shared and gagged over the stories of voyeurism and fondling from doctors, dentists, optometrists, you name it. It was close to impossible to find a female medical professional in those days, so we had few options. We hated going to the doctor, never knowing if he was "one of those."

One night, a friend told me a hair-raising story about a palsy she developed. I saw it when it happened and cringed for her—one half of her pretty face was paralyzed into a grimace for weeks. Already traumatized by this unsettling condition, she went to a doctor about it, hoping for his help. He told her to take off all her clothes and walk around his office naked, on her tiptoes, holding her arms over her head. He said this was how he conducted his examinations. She did it, because he was a doctor, right? But she burned with shame when she got it off her chest that night. We gasped at how dreadful that was, how wrong, how weird, but we didn't have any answers about what to do or how to protect ourselves in the future. He was the authority, a doctor, a man, and he knew what he was doing. And we acquiesced.

One episode happened to me during college, when a middle-aged doctor performed my routine annual pelvic exam. No one was else in the room in those days, just him and me.

He said, "I bet you have great orgasms," as he pinched my clitoris during the exam.

My mouth dried up, I couldn't speak, and my body stiffened. Then my old training to pretend nothing was wrong and to just go along with it kicked in again. I did the classic giggle: "Hee hee hee. Yeah, I do."

"I can tell," he said, as he proceeded to touch me and point out how my anatomy was arranged to make for good rubbing during intercourse.

And I just simpered, while inside I died. I got out of there as soon as I could, and of course never went back. I told my girlfriends later on, and again, they all said, "How awful. Yuck! You poor thing," and we just went on with our lives.

AFTER MR. DON fired me, I tramped door-to-door at restaurants until one offered me another waitress job, this time at a Greek establishment, of the dark, old-fashioned, businessman's club genre. When I arrived there the next week for my first day, the rules were different from what I had been told.

"When you're not serving drinks, you have to dance," the manager told me.

"What?"

"Yes, and here is your waitress and dance uniform," he said, as I gawked in horror at the tiny chiffon toga he handed me. It reminded me of what we called a "shorty baby-doll" nightgown—light yellow, filmy material hitting just inches below the crotch, leaving one shoulder bare.

I hesitated and worried, after what had happened with the motel maid uniform and the Mr. Don fiasco, *Will I have to model it for him? Does this sexy costume somehow imply sex with a manager like Mr. Don?* But I soldiered on. I needed the money to pay tuition.

I worked my butt off, showing up at ten thirty in the morning for dance practice before the restaurant opened. The other girls and I dress-rehearsed Greek folk dances, kicking and twirling in our togas. Then came the busy noon shift—lots of cocktails at lunch in this martini and vodka-with-a-twist kind of place. I put up with flirting and grabbing from the older male customers, who leered at me when I danced in between getting their drinks.

When lunch was over, the men stayed and drank until two or three; then I finally had a short break before happy hour. I would just put a coat over my toga and stroll around out in the sunshine, gobbling a quick sandwich.

Then it was back on from four in the afternoon to two in the morning, a long shift during which the touching and comments intensified and the demands for more dancing escalated as the drinking increased.

After about two straight weeks of this, I could hardly get out of bed and put on my Greek costume. My feet pained me from dancing in heels. But each day, there I was on the work schedule for all the shifts. Finally, I got up my nerve to ask the manager for a day off—and he fired me.

"But I've worked over two weeks straight and over eight hours a day without any breaks. I don't think that's even legal," I ventured. "Why are you firing me?"

"We just need a different type, a little sexier. We don't need to give you a reason—just go," he said.

Tearing up, I resorted to my default response: *What did I do wrong? Was it my boyish figure?* More young women today would know to say, "Screw him; that's ridiculous, and besides, 'sexy' was not a required skill listed for the job. This is illegal, so I think I'll call him on that." But in those days, spineless and too tired to protest further, I handed in my toga and slumped out the door.

I dragged myself into the university career center, hoping

for a miracle. Then I saw a California government job posted for a researcher needed to help farmers across the state with their pest problems. I dared to dream, *Perfect*. *This job fits my major, involves plants, and has a practical application with farmers, and I'll be outdoors—my favorite place. And I can quit my waitress life forever.* I rushed to fill out the application.

When I got the job, I performed cartwheels for an hour in the yard of my apartment building, finishing with a pirouette series. I began working for a PhD scientist, Dr. Terry Rawlins, an agricultural researcher who was becoming well-known. For my first role in my area of scientific interest, I showed up early each day, took on any odd job asked of me, and worked long hours unsolicited. We traveled around California and conducted research on all different kinds of crops, testing effects of weeds on production and examining various herbicide and weed-control treatments. It was so right for me; I thought it was my big break for sure. Usually there were several students and scientists on the field trips, so we had fun, too. I soaked up every bit of learning I could.

One summer day, Terry took just me out to do weed counts with him in a cornfield in central California. It was late in the afternoon, the sun-in-your-eyes, blinding part of the day, steamy hot—and a cornfield is one of the hottest places you can be in the summer, believe me. I was counting weeds in our research plots, going up and down the rows of corn, when I heard the dry corn leaves rustling, as they do with even the slightest wind gust. But the rustling was louder than usual. Then I heard it again and looked up. I saw Terry creeping around the cornfield, peeking down various rows. My hackles went up. But I ignored my instincts and continued my counts. Besides, clammy and itchy all over from the corn leaves, with my old jeans and raggedy long-sleeved shirt wet and stuck to my skin, I wasn't thinking about much else except getting finished and going home for a shower.

At last, we completed the work and climbed into the front seat of the white government pickup truck. Terry reached over, I thought to retrieve something from the glove compartment, but instead he grabbed me around the back of the neck and started kissing my face, filthy with peat dust. His stuck his tongue in my mouth and planted his dirty hand on my breast, squeezing. I nearly suffocated from the taste and texture of the black grit from the delta soil in his mouth.

Repulsed by his flushed face and body odor, by his audacity, by the whole thing, I pushed him away. He kissed me repeatedly, and I said, "No, no, no, you're my boss," but he continued his groping.

"Stop, stop." I was frantic. Finally, he quit and slumped down, staring out the front windshield.

"I've been married for seven years," he whined. "It's true what they say about the seven-year itch. I'm restless and bored. Things are bad, real bad. I just have to have more sexual experiences."

While he babbled about himself and his miserable life, I sat there in the pickup truck next to him, my heart hammering, desperate. This was my best job ever, and this was my boss, whom I had trusted and admired. My mind spun: *How could this be happening? What should I do? Is he going to fire me? I've got to fix this.*

With no skills or training in how to respond to sexual harassment, I could come up with only "Oh, that's okay. I understand."

I thought it was my job to smooth things over, make him feel better, make sure he wasn't angry, make it all right for him. And I didn't want to lose my job. I soothed him and patted his arm and said, "No problem. These things happen."

I listened to his tale of woe about his bad marriage. I had to make everything okay—that was what I'd been taught; those were my instincts. I certainly had no notion of how women should be treated or how to react in this kind of situation. I had been raised to believe that the man was always right, he had needs that he couldn't overcome, and the woman was inconsequential.

We rode home in silence. When he dropped me off, he told me, "Don't tell anyone," which definitely felt like a threat.

All night I tossed and turned. The next morning, I pulled myself out of bed, nervous for the workday to start. I rode my bike to campus and slunk into the lab—there were all my coworkers, and there was Terry. I peeked at him, but he leaned against the lab bench, chatting with his assistants, pretending nothing had happened. I went along with it.

"Good morning, Terry."

Of course, I never felt the same about the job or him. I remember feeling so disappointed and thinking, *Maybe I'm not really a good scientist after all. Maybe they keep me around only because I'm a girl and they like having a girl around, a plaything. I don't have the true skills needed for this job; my work is not stellar. I'm just a problem child. I'm always getting in trouble.*

But I didn't quit the job. My passion was to be a field biologist and a weed scientist, so I sucked it up.

A couple of years later, I attended a national science conference, where I won the award for best presentation by a graduate student. As I crossed through the restaurant in the hotel of the event, I saw Terry sitting on a stool with his cocktail. He motioned me over and said, "I want to thank you for not telling anyone."

"Yeah, sure," I said, ever the good sport, and walked away.

⌒

AFTER COMPLETING MY bachelor's degree in 1974, I applied for numerous professional positions in biology and botany. But after receiving the last rejection letter, I decided to pursue my master's degree. My first choice for my major professor was Dr. Bob Chandler, a big wheel in the weed-science community at the peak of his career. I told everyone about my good luck when I engaged him as my professor. "I'm going to become a weed expert, agriculturalist, plant physiologist—a real scientist! My professor is famous, and I'll learn so much from him. He's never had a 'girl' graduate student before. I'm his first one, so this is special for sure!"

In his office, overflowing with books and papers, I announced my academic plans as we began our collaboration. I worked for Bob during the school year and summers while I did my classwork and research. I worked hard, from dawn until way past dark, dirty in the field, with soil and plants. Riding my bike back and forth between campus and my apartment, I stood long hours at my lab bench and in the greenhouse, confirming my experimental results. It was strenuous work, but I tingled with satisfaction—and breathed more freely, since I was away from the job with Terry.

One day, Bob received a visit from the radioactivity police, a group that kept track of closely controlled radioactive substances around the university.

Bob's lab didn't pass inspection. He told the police, "It's because of my new graduate student, Lucinda. She spilled her radioactive materials all over the lab benches, and that's why our lab isn't clean. She's inexperienced and doesn't know any better yet."

It also came out during the inspection that Bob hadn't

renewed his radioactivity permit. He told the inspectors, "Lucinda was supposed to renew the permit and must have failed to turn in the proper paperwork."

They came into the lab and accused me. I stumbled over my words and knew he had lied to cover himself. But why had he blamed me? Because I was the girl, an easy target. He undermined me as a scientist and made me look careless and unprofessional. But he got away with it. I stood there next to the window in the white lab coat I was so proud of while the sun poured in on my plant experiments and these men chastised me for my poor training, bad technique, and late paperwork.

As soon as they left, I staggered to the bathroom and burst into tears, my heart cracking from the betrayal by my own professor, the scolding by other scientists, and the stares from the male graduate students in the lab. I wanted to shout out, "He's lying! Bob is a liar!" But I was afraid I'd lose my place in graduate school, afraid Bob would fire me or wouldn't sign off on my thesis—and plagued by many other fears and inner demons. So I kept quiet.

As I completed my research, I flung myself into writing my first publication. As the main author, I knew this was my "coming out" in the research community. I spent months perfecting my paper and proudly gave it to Bob for his review and approval. I waited and waited but heard nothing from him. The deadline drew near, then passed, for a scientific conference where I hoped to present my results. When I approached Bob again, he said he had submitted the paper for acceptance into the conference in time, so I heaved a sigh of relief.

At the conference, ready to present my paper, I stood, mouth agape, when Dr. Richard Ellis, the editor of the prized journal where I wanted to publish, came up to me and spat out, "I can't believe what you did just to get published—you women will do anything to get in. We pulled your paper from the conference and will not publish it."

I had no idea what he was talking about. What had I done? I charged frantically to Bob, and he told me, "Well, it's too bad, but the reviewers didn't like your paper. It wasn't up to their standards, so they rejected it."

"How is that possible? You reviewed the paper, too, and said it was ironclad. I worked so hard on that research to make it perfect. What were the reviewers' comments? When may I see the edits?" I pressed him, as I spiraled into a tailspin.

"Lucinda, they simply didn't like it. I can't show you the comments; they're confidential. Your paper is just unacceptable. Sorry."

After retreating to my hotel room for a bitter cry on my unmade bed, I sought out my friend Dr. Ben Adams, a professor at the same university as the editor, and told him what had happened. He related that, recently, Richard had come into his office with a piece of paper mostly covered up, with only a signature showing, and asked, "Is this your signature?"

It wasn't, so Ben replied, "No."

"I thought so," said Richard.

Later, Ben discovered and related to me that Bob had forged Ben's signature as a fake reviewer of my paper—apparently, Bob had missed the review deadline—so he just wrote in Ben's signature, claiming it had been peer reviewed, and sent it in to the editor. Of course, the editor assumed *I* had done it, not a prominent professor like Bob.

Accused of forgery, my paper withdrawn, I didn't get to present or publish my research. Over and over in my head, I said, *Will it never stop? But I won't let them crush me. I've worked too hard for this. I'm not in their club, but I'm not going away. I'll make my own club, even if I'm the only one in it.*

My determination stemmed partly from the fact that I saw field biologist researchers out there, having a great time, and I still wanted to be one of them. They had their own trucks and tractors, traveled around the country on their own schedule, received accolades for their contributions to science, and made good money to boot. Now that I was getting a taste of it, I thought, *I love this work. Outside in the breeze, clomping down the cotton rows, wearing my snakebite chaps, adding to science. I know there are no women doing this, but girls merit this kind of opportunity too. I deserve a fun, well-paid, challenging job, just like the men.*

With this daydream stowed in my pocket, I finished my Master of Science degree and headed out into corporate America.

SPROUTS OF LEGAL AND SOCIAL CHANGE

ALTHOUGH NEW LAWS were emerging around sexual harassment, they didn't do most of us any good in the early 1970s. And societal changes, like views on how men treat women, took years and years to reach an ordinary girl like me.

Though it wasn't discussed in the 1970s, the practice of using women as scapegoats, as my professor Bob did to me, is today defined as a form of sexual harassment. The modern behavioral-science definition of sexual harassment is "behavior that derogates, demeans, or humiliates an individual based on the individual's sex." Some people may take the idea of sexual harassment literally; however, sexual harassers are in fact driven not by sexual motives but "by a desire to protect and enhance their social status in the context of gender hierarchy." [1] Bob guarded his prestigious male role as professor by humiliating me and using a woman to take the blame and conceal his own incompetence.

What helped me most later on to figure out why all this exploded on me in the 1970s was a model about sexual harassment that Fitzgerald et al. developed in the '80s and '90s. The model resonated because it allowed me to put these incidents into "buckets." The researchers sorted sexual harassment into three categories:

1) *Gender harassment*: "disparaging conduct not intended to elicit sex" but rather "verbal, physical, and symbolic behaviors that convey hostile and offensive attitudes about women";

2) *Unwanted sexual attention*: "sexual advances that are inappropriate, unreciprocated, and/or offensive to the recipient (e.g., sexually suggestive comments, attempts to establish sexual relationships despite discouragement, unwanted touching)"; and

3) *Sexual coercion*: "subtle or explicit bribes or threats to make job conditions contingent on sexual behavior." [2, 3]

I saw that my father, my professor Bob, and camp director Roger were in the first bucket, gender harassment. My boss Terry in the cornfield belonged in the second category, unwanted sexual attention. My boy-manager at Roy Rogers was of the sexual-coercion persuasion in bucket number three. Others, like Mr. Don, were in all categories. The sexual harassment I received was all different, with slightly different motives, but this model gave me a platform to understand what these men were doing and how much of this was the same— about men and their power.

I also didn't realize I was working in some of the worst professions for harassment of women. The farms and fields where I worked in the 1960s and '70s, along with the motels and restaurants that employed me in the 1970s, are today considered the kinds of workplaces where women have suffered the most savage harassment and assault. Multiple studies and investigative reporting confirm that "female farmworkers face a real and significant risk of sexual violence and harassment," and, in a review conducted for more than a year, that "from the meat-packing plants of Iowa to the lettuce fields of California to the apple orchards of Washington, women expected to encounter sexual harassment, assault, and even rape at work." Women in the cleaning profession are "laboring in isolation for tiny paychecks"—a circumstance that leads to supervisor abuse, financial constraints, and shame that keep sexual harassment victims silent. [4]

Of any business in America, the restaurant industry has the highest percentage (37 percent) of sexual harassment complaints filed with the EEOC. As with my situation at Mr. Don's and at the Greek restaurant, women must live off tips and are often told to "go home and dress more sexy, show more cleavage," in order to sell more food and make higher tips. [5] It's also an early career job for young girls, which means our introduction into the work world includes extreme sexual behaviors by men that we learn early to tolerate and accept.

The rampant sexual harassment my female friends and I faced from medical professionals in the 1970s continues to rage in the 2010s. In 2016, investigators revealed thousands of cases of doctor sexual abuse in every state in America. The study discussed how vulnerable patients are, as they tend to be nervous and worried during a doctor visit, and how they trust a doctor, only to have that trust violated. Patients reported long-term effects, such as trauma, isolation, and complete avoidance of doctors in the future. The research also showed that these incidents are allowed to occur and doctors are not held accountable—they're rarely removed from practice, let alone disciplined. In 450 cases of doctors brought before courts and regulators for sexual misconduct from 2016 to 2017, half of those doctors still practice medicine. Even some who were criminally convicted are back in practice, within a system that obviously protects and pardons them. [6]

Few women held leadership positions in the early '70s. There were no women on the Supreme Court, only one female senator, and ten congresswomen. In her 1970 autobiography, *Unbought and Unbossed*, Shirley Chisholm, the first black US congresswomen, said that women "have cooperated in their own enslavement." She identified how it was difficult for women to become leaders because they "are taught not to rebel from infancy" and "have been programmed to be dependent on men." Socially, women were second-class citizens who, if they did work, earned about half the salaries of men. As was my experience in high school, Representative Chisholm noted that "guidance counselors discriminate against girls" as they steer them toward a dependent life, traditional education, and wife- and motherhood. She also realized that prejudice against women was widespread and said, "Being female put more obstacles in my path than being black" and, "This society is as antiwoman as it is antiblack." [7]

In 1972, the only S&P 500 company headed by a woman was the *Washington Post*, run by Katharine Graham. One. Woman. In all of corporate America. And I hadn't even heard of her. Graham herself was not liberated then either, commenting, "I adopted the assumption of many of my generation that women were intellectually inferior to men, that we were not capable of governing, leading, managing anything but our homes and our children." [8] Forty-six female employees filed a sex discrimination lawsuit against *Newsweek*, owned by the *Washington Post*, in 1970. Graham conceded that little action was taken, and in 1972, she received another round of complaints and an additional lawsuit against the *Post*. Even if the CEO was a woman, that didn't mean women were treated fairly in the workplace. Graham admitted she struggled with her own consciousness raising in the early '70s about women's issues, asking about the lawsuits, "What side am I supposed to be on?" [9]

On the other hand, some historical legal changes did occur during this era. In 1971, the Supreme Court decided its first sex discrimination case that utilized the 1964 Civil Rights Act and Title VII. The court ruled in favor of Ida Phillips, who had been denied employment because she was the mother of preschool-age children. Her case was declared discriminatory "because of sex," as the same rules did not apply to men with children that age.

As the women's liberation movement ramped up, women began challenging the American justice and societal systems. Although the term "sexual harassment" hadn't entered public parlance yet, a campaign against sexual advances in the workplace flowed out of legal disputes against sexual abuse and rape.

In 1972, the EEOC received authority to conduct its own enforced litigation, and women started coming forward with their cases. Another major milestone was Title IX of the Education Amendments issued in 1972. This prohibited sexual discrimination in federally funded education, including athletics. Later, Title IX was used as a basis for defining sexual harassment of students by teachers as illegal.

There were steps backward as well. In 1974, the district

court of the District of Columbia heard what is considered the first sexual harassment case. In *Barnes v. Train*, Paulette Barnes brought forth a claim when she was fired because she wouldn't sleep with her boss. However, the court decided this was not sexual discrimination or retaliation and dismissed her case. It stated that the boss simply found his employee attractive and that he was angry when she rejected his advances.

Sexual harassment finally got a name in 1975. A group of women at Cornell University supported a woman filing a claim for unemployment after she quit her job because her boss had touched her in a sexual way. Members of the group, called Working Women United, all shared similar experiences.

I didn't know anything about court cases or sexual harassment during this time, because most young college students like me were quite isolated politically and socially. We didn't have the Internet. The only way we heard news was from the newspaper or TV, neither of which I had as a poor graduate student. We had radio broadcasts, but mostly we listened to rock music, not news stations. As a science major, I discoursed with fellow students primarily about science, not current events, so I didn't hear about these changes going on for women. I ran all-consuming science experiments around the clock. I read constantly, but mostly science textbooks and scientific periodicals. The only journal I subscribed to was *Weed Science*.

I finally heard the term "sexual harassment" in 1977, when a woman friend handed me a copy of the latest *Ms.* magazine. My eyes were riveted to the cover: a businessman's hand crept down the front of the red dress of a female puppet office worker. The title screamed, "Special Report: Sexual Harassment on the Job and How to Stop It."

Wow! I thought. *Maybe this is what's been happening to me. What exactly is this? Why do men do it?*

A few years later, studies and research helped me to understand this phenomenon and to distinguish between two types of sexual harassment.

One type of sexual harassment occurs in the traditional women's job sector, such as the kind I experienced in the early 1970s when I was a motel maid and waitress. In 1978, Lin Farley said the purpose of this kind of sexual harassment was "to keep women down." [10] It usually involved forcing a woman to participate in unwanted sexual relations by threatening to get her fired if she didn't. It's a form of subjugation that attempts to restore male dominance over women, thus securing their power. Men see it as an opportunity to exploit a woman, since the man is usually in a superior position at work. Given the power dynamic, he thinks he can get sexual favors from women with whom he otherwise would not have a chance. This concept resonated with me, as the men who harassed me—usually married, unattractive, and older—were men I wouldn't have had anything to do with outside work. I see now that they used their positions as bosses to keep the power and sexual dynamic exactly the way they wanted it.

The second type of sexual harassment happens to women in nontraditional, typically male jobs. Farley sees this version as intended to "keep women out." It usually involves insults or mock proposals for sex with the purpose of showing contempt for a woman's "unfeminine" behavior, such as being in the workplace at all. Perpetrators of this kind of harassment are not really looking for sex—they just want to make a woman so uncomfortable that she'll quit. I saw this shift when I moved from part-time "women's" jobs into jobs—like my research positions with Terry and Bob—that men usually held.

This pattern only amplified in the late 1970s, as I crossed into the corporate world. However, additional distractions kept me from fully deciphering the mystery of sexual harassment. Nixon was in power, the Vietnam War flickered on every TV I passed by, and young adults my age during the early '70s ranted with placards, sit-ins, and marches against the government. We didn't trust anything the government was doing. Even if I had heard about new laws around sexual harassment, I probably would have scoffed and distrusted that politicians would ever enact them. We were antiestablishment and part of the "dropout" culture, particularly in California during the 1970s. From our perspective on the West Coast, Washington, DC, was far away and didn't involve us. We tuned out, hiking the redwood forests and backpacking in the Sierra Nevada. My jobs isolated me on Trout Lake in Maine, Mummy Island in Alaska, and the corn and tomato fields of California, so I wasn't exactly in a hotbed of current events.

Reed College was a liberal, freethinking school, but when protests and student meetings against the Vietnam War erupted, boys drove the movement while girls sat in the backseat in assistant roles, like getting coffee and sleeping with the boys. Nothing very antiestablishment about that.

One summer, a girlfriend of mine and I went hiking with two boys who asked us to take off our shirts and follow behind them without speaking for the rest of the day. It was some mountain-man, gender-role game we played that, at the time, evoked obvious subservient sensations in me. As my own consciousness was rising ever so slightly, I had an inkling that naked hiking and no talking, when only the girls were barebreasted and silent, might be considered sexist.

Despite all the wild-and-free slogans of the late 1960s and early '70s, it was really only wild and free for men. The hippie counterculture movement of the time was rife with harassment, sexism, and limited opportunities for women.

four

~○

KEEP US OUT

WHEN I WAS LOOKING FOR WORK AFTER COMPLETING MY master's degree in 1976, I found that most employers were accepting applications from women for traditionally male jobs—in many cases for the first time in their organization's history. I went on a whirlwind of interviews and received offers from several agricultural chemical companies.

My college dream of becoming a national park ranger was difficult to realize. There weren't many ranger jobs, they went mostly to men, and they didn't pay well. I was probably lucky in a way that these deterrents kept me from pursuing this line of work. In 2017, the National Park Service published an employee survey that revealed flagrant sexual harassment, going back decades, that no one had addressed. [1] I considered working in academia but found I had no options there without a PhD. I investigated positions at nonprofit organizations such as the World Wildlife Fund and government agencies like the fairly new Environmental Protection Agency Nixon formed in 1970. Those were possibilities, but the pay was low compared with what the chemical companies offered.

As an idealist and an environmentalist, I wanted to conserve the natural resources of the world. In my mind, ensuring the efficacy and safety of chemicals for plants, animals, and people was an effective way to help our planet. I decided to work from the inside of corporations, where I determined I could have the most impact. Sure, I could regulate chemicals through a government position or educate people on them from the classroom. But I sensed that sitting at the table, deliberating and deciding what chemicals, especially pesticides, a company was going to develop and produce in the first place, would be the most influential place to be. I could be that organization's conscience.

I accepted a position with a Fortune 500 chemical corporation as its first female field research biologist. Though this was a giant, East Coast-based chemical manufacturing company, it wasn't one of the big agricultural chemical players, but the job it offered me seemed ideal. Conducting research on the utility and environmental impact of pesticides (herbicides, insecticides, fungicides) in all crops (fruits, grains, vegetables, and more) across California, Nevada, and Utah, was an honorable endeavor. And I could continue living in California, where I had my family and my boyfriend. Like choosing Reed and Boston, I stuck with my theme of basing major personal decisions on the location of my latest boyfriend, even though the guys never lasted. But, with much hope, I put my life savings down on half a duplex on the outskirts of Davis, California, ready to settle into my new career position and my first real home of my own.

I didn't realize exactly what I was getting into at this first job. As I traveled to the offices, warehouses, and barns of agricultural chemical distributors and their farmer customers, I routinely faced calendars and photos of naked women posed on tractors, wearing overalls and no blouse, or sucking on a juicy apple from last year's crop. Entering these man caves, I carried on my business as best as I could while I stood there and pretended not to notice the female sex objects staring me in the eye. But the men would point them out anyway, just to make sure I didn't miss anything: "Hey, look at Miss October!"

I also got lots of "What are you doing here, missy?" and "You sure don't look like a scientist, sweetheart," and so on, reinforcing that I was invading their male territory.

There was even a farmer who, hoping to drive me off his land, intentionally didn't call off his dog. It chased me and bit me in the butt as I desperately tried to leap back into my company pickup truck, ripping my favorite jeans and drawing blood, while the farmer stood there and snickered. I had to leave work to get a tetanus shot.

Farmers did a double take when they spotted me approaching their field, and their wives raised their eyebrows if I climbed up to the porch and knocked on the door of the farmhouse. They were conservative, no doubt, as was evident when I sat in the over-upholstered living room of one farmer and his wife for cookies and coffee, with the TV on in the middle of the day. Joan Baez came on the screen, and the farmer warned me that she was a "pinko."

Besides the conservatism, which I could manage, many of them were respectful. They had wives as partners and daughters who helped out on the farm, so, on some level, I felt marginally accepted. Even though for them I was an oddity, and they sometimes challenged my right to be there, they didn't use the sexual harassment weapon the way, it turned out, my corporate peers did.

One day, a friendly male colleague and I were dawdling in the local farmer diner over a cup of coffee and I asked him straight out, "Why don't my peers, bosses, and senior colleagues want me here? They're hostile. The farmers don't seem as angry about my presence as my company cohorts."

He said something I just hadn't thought of: "Because

you're a competitor to the company folks, and a good one. They feel threatened. You may get the top job rating they covet. You might get that promotion they expect for themselves. They may be ruthless in their attacks to eliminate you as a rival."

It wasn't something I had grasped before. As I woman, I hadn't been taught to compete. I was a team player, a collaborator, a friend. It hadn't occurred to me that my colleagues and I were competing. I had much to learn about the man world.

When my company reorganized for strategic purposes and disbanded its Northern California research department, it compensated me with a job offer as a pest control advisor and sales representative to local farmers in Southern California. My sister, Deborah, and I traveled there for a trial visit and house-hunting trip, as she was thinking of going to the nearby university.

I accepted the job and found a suitable home in the nearby town of Santa Barbara. But when I phoned my prospective boss, Dick, a big, burly man's man, with my news about the house, he began a rant that went like this: "You can't live in that town. If *I* can't afford to live there, you have no business living there. Besides, women shouldn't be in these jobs anyway, and I'm only hiring you because they're making me do it. I don't want you or any woman here. And I'm not the only one. None of us do."

"Well, Dick," I choked out, stuffing my immediate impulse to cry with the hurt he laid on me, "You've put it right out there, loud and crystal clear. I don't know what to say. I'll have to think about all this. I'm sorry."

Later, Deborah and I lay on a Santa Barbara beach, hot and deserted midday, trying to relax. After her visit to the campus, the college scene had little appeal to my sister. I squirmed around, replaying Dick's verbal assault in my head. We squinted at each other across our beach towels and simultaneously came to the conclusion: "Let's get out of here."

We left on the next flight.

The next day, jittery about my job and money and Dick's reaction, I steeled myself to call back East to the company headquarters. I told them, "Maybe this isn't going to work. Dick doesn't seem to like me and doesn't want me or any woman to work for him."

They got a lawyer on the phone immediately and then found a job for me in Northern California. The attorneys obviously knew the laws around harassment and discrimination, while I didn't. I'm sure they were relieved that I was uninformed and unassertive.

The small farm town I moved to for my new position appealed to me. It was apple country, and during harvest in the fall, the town bustled with the processing of the fruit at the local plant and a delicious apple-pie scent filled the air. My job was in sales, as a pest control biologist and advisor to the grape, apple, prune, and other fruit growers in Sonoma and Napa Counties. It wasn't in research, my first love, but it was still a way to protect the environment by minimizing pesticide use and guiding farmers toward organic farming, which was just taking off in California. I took the job and, at twenty-five years old, moved there in early 1977.

Wally, the gray-haired biologist whom I replaced, was retiring. When I first moved to town, he and his wife left on vacation for a month. In a genial gesture, they invited me to stay in their home until I could find a place to live. Their old house sat out in the country on an apple farm, quaint and homey in the daytime, the adjacent apple orchard blooming cheerfully in the California sun. But at night, with no nearby neighbors, the isolated house creaked when the wind picked up, and the apple trees rustled and groaned.

Part of the deal was that I took care of their two cats while they were out of town. When one of the cats gagged and spit up, I found a veterinarian in the phonebook who wasn't too far away and rushed the cat to see him. Filling out the paperwork with all my information—name, address, phone number—I chatted to the vet about how I lived alone out at Wally's place.

That night, the phone rang. When I answered, a male voice said, "How is your cat?" He quickly hung up. Then he called again and again. We were conditioned in those days of few phone calls and no answering machines to always pick up the phone. I thought, *Don't answer it. It's probably him again. But it might be someone else. It might be my mom, it might be one of my farmer clients, it might be important, I have to answer.* But each time, it was the vet, and his comments escalated from "I want you" to "I know where you live" to "I know you're alone."

This was not the first time this had happened to me. Though I had found my first obscene phone caller, when I was nine years old, oddly validating, I had lived protected back then in my parents' womb. This time, alone and savvier, I felt terror surge under my rib cage. I locked all the doors and windows, put a chair behind the door in my bedroom, and made an unsuccessful stab at sleeping. I heard every rattle and wind gust all night long.

The next day after work, I drove around late into the night to avoid Wally's house, with a pit in my stomach that wouldn't subside. But I had nowhere else to go, so I finally pulled as quietly as possible into the gravel driveway, crept into the house, and readied myself for bed. Just as I started to relax a little, the phone rang and the same voice said, "I'm going to have sex with you." He hung up, then called again and told me,

"I'm coming to get you." Another hang-up, then the call where I finally screamed, before he could disconnect, "Stop calling me! I know who you are! I'm calling the police!"

He replied, "I'm going to kill you."

I slammed down the phone and hurled myself around the house, yanking down all the shades, and howled into the empty rooms, "Oh my God, oh my God, oh my God." I dialed the police and then the only person I knew in town, Saul, the warehouseman at work who had become a kind of friend. When two policemen finally arrived in their patrol car, I told them about the cat and the veterinarian and they promised to investigate, but that did not relieve my panic. I calmed down a little when Saul and his wife dispatched their two teenage boys to stay with me for the night.

The next day, when I called the police again to check on actions, they said, "Well, there is a vet here in town who is slightly off. We've had reports about him. But, you know, his parents are rich and important here in our community, so we aren't going to make a big deal about this." The teen boys, awkward and shuffling in the living room and dying to go home, stayed with me for a few days until I found a new place to live in town, in a busy apartment complex.

I buried myself in my job to try to erase the whole episode, but my new boss, Lonnie, wouldn't let me forget that my gender made me a sitting duck in the workplace as well. He announced at the office to anyone who would listen, "I don't think women should work in men's jobs. They're stealing work from married men with families."

Then he accused me of cheating on my expense report. "Lonnie," I protested, "are you kidding me? I would never do that. In fact, here are all my receipts from that day; you can see I was in Healdsburg and bought my lunch. I charged the

$2.50 for it right here. It's hard proof nothing is out of order."

Lonnie's eyes shone with excitement as he said, "Glen bought your lunch that day. It's on his expense report, so you cheated the company out of $2.50. You'll be fired for this." He never vindicated me, even when Glen came forward and said he had made a mistake and entered our lunch together on his report on the wrong day.

Since the cheating accusation wasn't successful for him and he couldn't fire me for it, Lonnie charged me with having an affair with the warehouseman—Saul, the same generous man who had sent his teenage boys to protect me. Lonnie called Saul's wife, Sandy, on the phone and told her, "You know how sometimes Saul comes home late from work? Well, he and Lucinda have a secret meeting place in the back of the warehouse, and after work they get it on together back there. This has been going on since she arrived here."

When Saul told me about this accusation, I felt sick to my stomach. We both shook our heads and stared at the ground, scraping our feet around in the dirt outside the warehouse. Thankfully, Sandy didn't believe it. She and I talked, and she said she knew it was a sick lie. Lonnie was using any ploy he could find to drive me off.

At the time, I just didn't get it. I thought, *This is horrific. Why is he after me? Why is he fabricating this?* I didn't know about harassment as a war instrument, didn't realize to what lengths men would go to discredit and keep women out of what they considered men's work, until I saw Anita Hill ripped apart on TV in 1991. I didn't fathom back in the '70s that Lonnie could use tactics such as smearing my reputation or accusing me of promiscuity to conspire to fire me or make me quit. I was the top salesperson in the region that year, which must have irked him.

It didn't occur to me until quite recently that my former prospective boss Dick, in Southern California, must have set Lonnie against me. At the time, I had no concept of the old boys' network and how it worked. Today, I know Dick contacted Lonnie, mad as hell because I had gotten him in trouble, and told Lonnie that I needed to go. So the vendetta started right away—I had no chance. I thought that by leaving Southern California, I was leaving all of Dick's prejudices behind me and could move on. I didn't realize then how things worked, but now I know that the lawyers and human resources specialists talked to Dick about his behavior. And of course he denied it but sought his revenge through Lonnie's retaliations.

At that point, I searched for a new job and another Fortune 500 company offered me a research and development position in 1978, again as the first female field biologist in its history. This was more of a life sciences company than my previous employer, producing chemicals, food additives, polymers, and pharmaceuticals. It was starting to work in agricultural chemicals, especially herbicides, and was on its way to becoming a big player in the agricultural chemical world. I would live in Missouri, near the world headquarters, while waiting for my field assignment.

My feelings about the previous few months pulsed helter-skelter in my heart and head. On the one hand, on hearing the news about my new job, I drove to the beach and did my leap series over and over in the sand—one-legged leap, stag leap, two-legged leap—to celebrate my freedom from sexist Dick and Lonnie. On the other hand, I cringed, back in my living room, thinking, *I hate that those two men got the better of me and made me quit. They got what they wanted—I'm leaving. They were successful in their methods, and now they can go safely back to their man world. And what if they victimize the next woman, like they did to* me? *I'm not helping her. And what if it happens again in my new job?*

But, forever the optimist, I flipped Stevie Wonder on my turntable and waltzed around my apartment to "Isn't She Lovely," cheering my return to my chosen field of research, instead of marketing. And this job was a chance to work in corn and soybeans, the big-ticket crops, experimenting with new herbicides in the field. There was a kind of maxim that if you hadn't worked in corn and beans, you just didn't know the US ag market—so I needed to punch that ticket. Also, I took the job because it meant I could see my new long-distance boyfriend, Ron, who lived in Texas, more often. Ron and I had met when I waded into a rice paddy in my hip boots; he was an agricultural corporate type like me, out assessing crops in the field. I figured the Midwest was closer to Texas than California, so we might get together more regularly. My relocation would also uphold my pattern of culling jobs based on boyfriends.

Before I started my new position, I moved to Texas for a couple of months to be with Ron. I fantasized that he was "the one." Just as I had with boys in high school, I thought if we had sex, it meant love, and love meant marriage. But this time, my dreams of marriage reached new heights: *We'll be apart for a while, but we're in love, love, love and we can work it out. I'll move to Texas full-time eventually and we'll get married and I'll wear a LUCINDA belt along with cowboy boots and a cowboy hat like he does and it will be so wonderful. Or, better yet, if I play my cards right, I won't even move to the Midwest. He'll ask me to marry him and I'll just stay in Texas.*

I wanted him to meet my mother, since marriage was in the fairyland in my head, even though Ron and I hadn't talked about that level of commitment. To try to capture the mood of him, I told my mom that Ron and I had a special album—Billy

Joel's *Stranger*—which I played for her to symbolize our budding relationship. She sat still in the chair in my living room with a forced smile on her face as she listened to the music. Her only comment was "That's nice." She didn't want to meet him. She knew more than I did, must have sensed the relationship might be fleeting. I wish she could have warned me somehow, and that I had listened.

Sure enough, Ron didn't propose and didn't ask me to stay in Texas. But I didn't give up hope, thinking, *He just needs a little more time. I'll go ahead and move to Missouri, and he'll miss me every second. He'll realize how much he loves me. I still love him with each inch of my soul. We didn't break up; he's just my boyfriend, rather than my fiancé, right now. We can work it out because we'll still see each other and talk on the phone all the time.*

I LAUNCHED INTO my research position at my new company, where Dr. Greg Stewart was the head of the research and development program. All the field biologists reported indirectly up to him, so he was my boss's boss. I can still picture him with his all-male underlings gathered around him at the coffeepot in the morning. He regaled them with witty stories featuring him, and his minions guffawed, whether his anecdotes were funny or not.

Greg had brought me to the headquarters until I was sent to the field somewhere in the United States. Around five o'clock each work evening, divorced and bored, he would roam around the office, saying, "Let's go out for drinks. I'm buying!" He'd stop by my cubicle and persuade me to join in, too: "Aw, come on, it's quittin' time! It's happy hour, and we can eat hors d'oeuvres for free. I call that dinner!"

It's nice to be included, I thought the first time he asked.

But the evenings never matched my vision of good company, nice conversation, and career advice. Rather, everyone drank too much, Greg demanded all the attention, there was lots of guy talk about sports and women, and, at the end of the night, I unlocked the door to my single apartment feeling lonelier than I'd been when I'd left. I didn't want to go to any more compulsory parties after the first experience but felt obligated to attend Greg's entourage gatherings when I couldn't think of an obvious excuse to decline.

After I had been working at the company for a few months, Greg started pressuring me to go out with him. "How about just the two of us get together tonight? How about coming over to my apartment for a drink? I know you're going to the conference in Toronto, since I just approved your participation, so let's meet up there. Yeah, I know you say you have a boyfriend, but he lives seven hundred miles away."

I continued to swear loyalty to Ron; besides, I knew from the way Greg talked about her that he was also obsessed with a young, beautiful, up-and-coming woman at the company, named Suzanne. He related, "Suzanne is so smart. She can really run a meeting. She has all the guys eating out of her hands. She's gorgeous, too. And tough. We have such a blast together; we see each other all the time. She's so funny and clever, she can tell a joke almost as well as I can!"

Yet one time when I spent the night at Suzanne's house, she confessed, "Lucinda, Greg is badgering me with constant phone calls, pretenses of meetings that don't exist, drop-ins. My boyfriend told him to stop, but he won't. Greg came by last night again unexpectedly and tried to kiss me, and I couldn't get rid of him. It's awful. I feel so guilty and ashamed. And I'm afraid for my job. He's an executive; he has a lot of influence over my career. And he's untouchable."

It was just what he was starting to do to me. We gushed out our stories, but neither of us knew what to do. We kept quiet and never talked about it again.

GREG DECIDED TO send me to the heart of the Midwest, Decatur, Illinois. It wasn't far from the world headquarters where he was located, so he could "keep an eye on me," as he said.

Decatur, a rough farming town called the Soybean Capital of the World, was not a healthy place for a single, twenty-seven-year old woman in 1978. The air hung heavy with the smell emanating from the soybean factory that towered over the town, looking like the *Daily Planet* building from *Superman*. The smell started out pleasing, like baking bread, then evolved into a sickeningly sweet odor that you couldn't get away from, no matter where you went. It was freezing, pipe-breaking cold in the winter, and hot as hell in the summer. Men in pickup trucks threw beer cans at me when I jogged, and the neighbors' kids always asked me, "Where is your husband?"

When I first arrived at the office to meet the rest of the Illinois team, there were big sighs of relief from the all-male group gathered around the conference table. When I asked why they were saying "whew" and "thank God," one man finally told me, "Well, not only did we think a woman was coming, which was bad on its own, because we've never worked with one before, but we also figured you were black because you have a black name—Jackson. We couldn't have handled it. This will be tough enough."

Wow, I thought. *What a welcome. They're saying they don't particularly want to work with a woman, just like Dick at my last job—and on top of that, they're racist, too? How am I ever going to survive here?*

As I shared my misgivings with my sister, Deborah, she proposed that she and our honorary sister, Linda, come out from California to help me adjust. They always listened and said, "What the fuck?" and, "Oh my God!" and commiserated about how some of the things happening to us just weren't right. I knew a visit from them would set me straight, though it ended up that even more weirdness reared its nasty head.

We cruised around in my big maroon company sedan in the central Illinois countryside, where endless fields of corn and soybeans dominated the scenery. I loved the tough, waving cattle-feed "dent corn," so named for the small dent in each kernel, as distinguished from sweet corn, which had softer, smooth kernels. I also had a fondness for round brown soybean seeds, processed for their oil and into high-end animal feed, that were like little bouncing eyeballs when broken from their pods.

Deborah, Linda, and I were an anomaly by central Illinois standards: three "older" single women out on our own. Most women in that area sported big diamond wedding rings on their fingers and toted three kids by age twenty-two. When we left my company car outside a small roadside restaurant while we ate breakfast, someone wrote "suck a boob" on the driver's side in white paint, I guess just to harass three young women alone. What did that even mean, anyway? They wanted to suck our boobs? We should suck each other's boobs? We tried to rinse it off, with no success, so we had to drive around in the frosty fall Midwest morning with the painted slur on the driver's window. When a policeman stopped me for speeding, I quickly rolled down the window. That hid "suck" but left "a boob" still visible on the driver's side back window. I lowered my eyes and hung my head, as if it were my doing, while the officer wrote my ticket. He made no comment, but in my quick glances toward him I could see his eyes flickering back and forth between me and that window like a front-row fan at a tennis match. Was this our scarlet letter *A*?

A few days later during their visit, I experienced sharp pains in my stomach that intensified into the evening. Frightened, Deborah and Linda drove me to the dilapidated emergency room at the old hospital in town. We entered the long, low-ceilinged corridor, where only one other patient, who was obviously delusional, waited. Clothes rumpled, hair wild, she shrieked, "Right quick, right quick, I gotta get out of here right quick!" I knew how she felt.

When the doctor finally called me in, he barked out a few questions and examined me clothes on, then ordered a prescription. When I asked him what the diagnosis was and what the drugs were for, he ignored me. I shuffled out, confused, waited for my prescription, and tried again questioning the pharmacist, especially after I saw the big sack filled with horse pills. He said roughly, "Just take them!"

I found a female nurse and asked her what was going on.

She took me aside and whispered, "You have VD."

What? I knew I didn't. I hadn't been with anyone; there were no dates for me in Illinois. We realized it was totally a sexist assumption: I was from California, single, young, so these moralistic male doctors judged me with their prejudices against women and sealed my case. But they were too squeamish even to talk about it.

The pains went away by morning. Years later, after I had repeated incidences of these stomach problems, I finally visited an internist, who, after many tests, diagnosed that I was unable to digest the carbohydrates in nuts. Deborah, Linda, and I had eaten a family-size bag of peanuts that night. How many other male doctors have misdiagnosed and mistreated women with their erroneous condemnations and suppositions? The whole experience smacked of "hysteria" and "nervous conditions" for which women were given drugs or sent away to sanatoriums by male medical professionals in decades past.

EVEN THOUGH I devoted myself to the cause—writing love letters, placing long-distance phone calls, flying wherever I could meet him—the Midwest–Texas romance between Ron and me fizzled. We had rendezvoused in New Mexico, Louisiana, New Jersey, Texas, Colorado, and so on, drifting along until gradually his already scanty communications and visits waned to nothing. Though divorced, Ron then told me that he and his ex-wife had reunited. I masked my loneliness and heartache with ceaseless activity: ice sailing, flying lessons, tennis, racquetball—anything to keep busy.

Like a master puppeteer playing with his puppets, Greg sent a tall, good-looking young college man to be my summer intern. When he made the announcement to me, Greg had a distinctive gleam in his eye, but I didn't take the time to decipher it that summer while Bill and I worked each day together out in the hot Illinois sun and humidity, I in my bathing suit top and jeans, he shirtless in the corn and soybean fields. I fell in love with my intern, who was all for it. Once again, even though Bill never told me he loved me, I pictured a romantic courtship—love and sex and happiness—that culminated in marriage. *Even though he's almost ten years younger than I am, we can make this work. I know he hasn't finished college, but we can commute back and forth while he completes his degree, and then we can get married. It'll be exciting and romantic. I can help him, be his support and muse.* Then Bill told me one night when we were in bed together that he was going to ask his virgin high school sweetheart to marry him.

Tears streamed down my face as I rolled off the bed, grabbed my jeans, and shouted for him to get out. My heart swelled with hurt and hardened at once. I thought, *What is he doing in bed with me? I thought he loved me. How could he have been so dishonest? He was just playing with me. I should never have trusted him.* Soon afterward, he left the internship and went on to marry his girl.

Greg probed, asking endless personal questions about my relationship with Bill that summer, until I cracked and told him that Bill and I were in fact dating. Bill turned out to be an old friend of Greg's, so, even though I was in the dark, Greg knew all along about the high school paramour. Greg informed me later that he had wanted to experiment with me and observe how a woman performed in a man's job. "I sent Bill there as a test to see what you would do. I have to say, I got a kick out of watching all that," he said.

Functional by day, I sobbed at night in my Decatur house, where I lived alone—for the heartbreak and the fact that my boss awarded himself vicarious thrills at my expense. It had all been staged, and I had fallen for it.

Around my first anniversary in the Illinois office, the company moved three under-twenty-five-year-old female sales representatives to three different towns around the state. *Finally, some relief,* I thought. *As the research and development rep, I'll be working closely with them on technical issues. This is thrilling—to have possible friends, comrades, other women!* But the corporation set them up to fail.

One was a tall, stunning black woman, fashion-model beautiful, whom the company located in an all-white farming community that still had a branch of the Ku Klux Klan. She endured countless racial and sexual taunts on the street and finally, understandably, quit. The other two, Gayle and Marilyn, were former school teachers with no marketing experience, and the company did nothing to train them, just threw them out there on their own into a hostile, male environment. The women were programmed for defeat, so if they quit, too, the managers could say, "See, just as we told you, women can't do these jobs. We tried—we hired women, like we were supposed to—but they just can't handle men's jobs."

Marilyn resigned after a month. Gayle, young and enthusiastic, stayed on and tried hard to do a top-notch job. One early evening, she and I visited a farmer's field to examine a low spot in his acreage where particularly troublesome weeds were competing with his soybeans. He drove us out to the swampy area in his pickup and kept us standing there for about an hour while it got dark. As he chatted, mosquitoes swarmed all over us, biting us dozens of times, until bumps mushroomed on our arms and faces. While we were scratching ourselves, he stood there, untouched and relaxed.

When we got back to his truck, he pulled out a can of insect repellant and smirked, "Want some?"

It dawned on us that this had been a test just to fuck with us. Gayle quit within a week after that, but I hung on.

RON AND I decided to give our relationship another go. Most of the enthusiasm was on my part, though I yo-yoed. Ron and his ex-wife had been on-again off-again ever since he and I had broken up, but he said, "We split up for good this time. I'm a free man."

I still love him, I thought. *But he rejected me. But I need him! Maybe he's changed. Maybe we can still follow the "happily ever after" scenario that I dreamed about. But I hope he and his ex-wife are really over each other. I want to try again.* We hatched a romantic plan to meet in Connecticut, since Ron was going there on a business trip. Ron's boss, Dr. Tom Silverton, was flying from Texas in his private plane and offered to pick me up in Illinois and fly me to his house in Connecticut, where Ron and I were going to stay for a night. *How thrilling,* I thought. *Not only will I see Ron tonight, but Tom said I could fly his plane—a perfect addition to my flying lessons.* I danced around and practiced new song lyrics in my head while waiting in the empty terminal for Tom to arrive at the small local airport.

After the excitement of flying the plane and buzzing across the country dwindled, Tom engaged the autopilot and we were quiet, the murmur of the engine the only sound. I fell asleep. When I woke up, Tom's hands were inside my blouse, massaging my breasts. My mind raced: *Oh my God. What the hell? This is my boyfriend's boss. He's married. His wife is meeting us at the airport. This is horrible. He's piloting this plane; my life is in his hands. What am I going to do?*

I squirmed away from him as best I could in the small cockpit and yelped for him to stop, though what I really wanted to do was smash him in the face. Tom laughed like it was nothing. My heart banged in my chest for the rest of the trip. I watched every move he made and stayed wide awake, super alert for any more weirdness, until we finally landed in Connecticut. Tom's wife and Ron met us at the airport, and we all exchanged well-bred greetings. Then we headed back to their established suburban home.

I told Ron about it that night when we were finally alone in the guest room, but he didn't really say much, just "oh" and "uh-oh." I'm not even sure he believed me. Men do not like to hear about other men's bad behavior, especially at work, where they really stick together. Tom was Ron's supervisor, after all. On the one hand, there was his girlfriend, with an ugly accusation against his boss. On the other hand, there was his boss, who represented his career, raises, promotions, and male camaraderie. Ron chose to believe the best of Tom.

I pretended to be sick so I wouldn't have to see Tom or his wife in the morning, though I wasn't really faking, because I did feel rotten inside. I slept all day in the guest bed to avoid any contact. When Ron and Tom returned in the evening from their business meetings, I emerged and faced them, and we all had dinner together, but I was too much of a nervous wreck to eat. Then, finally, Ron and I left, having said nothing about the "incident."

Ron and I broke up again. You'd think it happened because he didn't support me when his manager attacked me, but no, it was because he started having an affair with the woman who lived across the street from him in Texas and broke my heart.

I had been conflicted about love, sex, and marriage forever. In childhood, Deborah and I made elaborate weddings out of hollyhocks—complete with bride and groom, bridesmaids, groomsmen, and ring bearers—and our dolls were forever staging nuptials. We heard constantly, "Marriage is the goal for girls. If you go to college, it's to meet your future husband. If you didn't score in college, go get a job to try to find one there."

I flashed back to high school and the groom I made out with on his wedding night, and how sure I'd been that he would break it off and marry me. I looked at every man that way—as a potential spouse. Even though my parents' marriage hadn't worked out, I still put the institution up on a pedestal, albeit a teetering one. And the messages from the '50s combined with the liberating messages of the '60s into a huge, conflicting mess in my head. *The goal is to get married, but the '60s told me I should embrace free love/sex. I want men to like me, so I'd better have sex with them and show them I'm modern. But I want them to marry me, so sex has to mean marriage. Love means sex, which means marriage, right? And they wouldn't have sex with me unless they loved and respected me, right? I'm a good girl. But Bill wanted to marry a virgin! I'm not a virgin, but if they marry me, then that will sanction the sex I had with them.* But it didn't seem to be working out that way as I mourned another loss, playing Billy Joel again and again and crying nightly for weeks.

IT WAS A lonely time at the company, too. At big corporate events, I had to brace myself while pausing outside a banquet room, gearing up for cocktail hour. I knew that there were two hundred men inside and that when I, the only woman, stepped in, the chatter would quickly subside while they gawked at me. I would have to survive the gauntlet across the silent room to get my rum and Coke at the bar, until someone had the guts to talk to me. There were fishing trips I wasn't invited to, hunting weekends that went on without me, company dinners and golf outings for the men only. It was almost worse when I *was* invited—twenty men on a fishing boat in Wisconsin on which I was the only woman, everyone drunk and putting an arm around me by nine in the morning.

Corporate events with wives included were always awkward. I felt as if I should mix with the women, but often their talk was about children and home, things I couldn't relate to at that point in my life. It was a tough balancing act, back and forth, trying to please everyone and fit in somewhere. On one occasion, I asked one of my colleagues, "How is your new assignment in Kazakhstan?"

"Oh, just super. The job is fantastic, and my wife and I love the place!"

A few minutes later, I found myself with his wife, who confided in me, "If we move one more time, he's going by himself. I am so sick of this life, and now we're in Atyrau, and I hate it."

My head spun. Ultimately, I wanted to talk with the men, since for me these events were about projects and careers. That's what we were there for; this was work, after all. But I was continually faced with the pitfalls of trying to bond with my male workmates, even the seemingly harmless and decent ones. At one of our global corporate meetings, where meals were always mandatory, I was at breakfast one morning with all men, including my fatherly boss, Dr. Doug Norman, when one man ordered fried eggs. Someone snickered; then they all busted up laughing. I looked over curiously at Doug and saw him, whom I trusted, chuckling too.

"You guys, what's up? What's so funny?" I asked, but they all snorted again, not answering. I felt my face flush with embarrassment, then anger, as it became obvious that something inappropriate was happening and I was out of the loop.

Later, I approached one of my colleagues to ask what the joke was about. He hesitated, then said, "Your nickname is Fried Eggs."

"What?"

"Yeah," he said. "It's because you're so flat-chested that your breasts look like fried eggs."

After all these years, a shudder goes through my body when I recall that conversation. There was the additional blow that my supervisor was in on it—another moment when someone I considered my friend, on my side, let me down.

At another event, in a depressing little town in the Midwest, after grinding through our long meetings, we adjourned for an obligatory group dinner, which always seemed to be roast beef. Instead of just wearing my boxy maroon business suit and beige blouse to the meal, I saw it as an opportunity to dress up.

The week before, my mother had come to visit me and wanted to help me pick out a dress for my business trip. A home economics major in college, she had never been in the business world, but she loved pretty clothes and good fabric. In one shop, she found a shiny purple dress with a full slit down the left leg that tied up with black laces. A little racy in my mind, but it was high-necked and long-sleeved, and she was conservative in her light blue cotton blouses, little beige slacks, and white sweaters. If my mother approved, it must be okay.

"You've got to try this on," she exclaimed. "A young lady should dress up for dinner."

When I came out of the dressing room, she said, "Oh, how darling that looks on you. I wish I were tall and thin like you. You've got to get it."

I packed it for my trip and decided to wear it for the after-work function that night. Once again, my entrance into the room was the hardest part because I knew one hundred men and no other women were clustered inside, but I muscled open the big doors and strode into the hotel conference room laid out for dinner. All conversation stopped as I crossed the floor to find my seat. I trembled a bit with all those eyes on me, but I made it, found my nameplate, sat down at my designated spot, and started a conversation with the nearest person about our latest research trials.

Drs. Joe Camden and Len Colletti, two of my coworkers at the conference, asked me to go have drinks after the long, boring meal. They were both married, so I figured their intentions were good. Joe was kind of a mentor to me and had a wry sense of humor that I appreciated. The best advice he ever gave me was "If you want people in the office to think you're important, just grab a piece of paper and run like hell."

So I thought, *How nice. They're both older and higher up than I am—good folks to schmooze with about business. It's a chance to talk about work and maybe advance my career, so, sure, I'll go with them. They're like big brothers who are interested in my scientific and research abilities.*

We sat at a small table in the smoky hotel bar. Tinkly jazz piano filled the room.

"Can I buy you a drink?" Joe asked, and we all chuckled because we knew it was on his expense account.

Later, after a couple of cocktails, he leaned over and asked, "Want to dance?" He pulled me up from my chair and brought me in close.

Whoa, what's this? I thought. *But wait, I'm safe—he's my friend.*

I enjoyed the music and even put my sleepy and somewhat inebriated head on his shoulder for a second. It had been an exhausting day of holding my own among all those men.

We returned to our table and talked about the conference and our careers—all business again. This was just what I'd hoped for—older colleagues to show me the corporate ropes. But it was getting late and we had more meetings in the morning.

Joe said, "How about if we walk you home?"

I protested, "There's no need. It's just upstairs. I can manage," but they came along anyway. I thought it was sweet of them—old-fashioned for sure, but nice.

As we approached my door, I said, "Good night. Thanks, guys." But they stuck around as if they wanted to make sure I got in safely.

When I put my key in the lock and opened the door, they shouldered their way into my room.

My pulse raced. "What are you doing?" I asked.

A chill penetrated all the way to my bones as they locked the door behind them and announced, "We aren't leaving until you have sex with us."

"No, no," I said, as they pushed me onto the shiny hotel bedspread and stood over me. I crumbled, scrunched myself up smaller and smaller, my stomach and chest churning. I thought, *What about the brotherly advice you gave me? I thought we were friends. I thought you wanted to help me. Are you going to rape me?* I started to cry.

They loomed over me for what felt like hours, watching me as I shook with fear and shame, begging them to leave. Finally, Len said, "She's not going to do it. Let's go." And they sauntered out the door, banging it behind them.

I cried on and off all night as I kept waking up and going over it in my head: *Was it all my doing? When I put my head on his shoulder, was that the downturn? Was I asking for it? Was it my purple dress? Did Mom betray me? I trusted her opinion—why didn't she protect me? I'm a fool, naive, a mess. It's all my fault.*

But somehow, morning came. I got up, put on the standard, shapeless business suit I'd packed, this time in gray, and shoved open the hotel room door. I made it down the hall, into the elevator, across the lobby, and into the meeting room. There were Joe and Len, laughing it up with their male colleagues. They didn't look up, even though I stared pointedly their way to see if they would display any hint of remorse, embarrassment, apology. But no, nothing.

I engaged quickly with others, saying, "How's your morning? Good meeting yesterday," while thinking, *I've got to get through this. They won't drive me out. I'm burning up with shame, good God, but I'm back to work.*

My ability to compartmentalize saved me professionally. It allowed me to perform at studying, tests, and work, even after a night like that one. I could always remove distasteful events to different parts of my brain, secluding them there while I zeroed in on my job. The more I practiced this mental sequestration, the easier it was.

That didn't mean I didn't feel it, though. My life consisted of lots of long, weepy phone calls with my sister and friends to go over every injustice—but these talks allowed me to get it out so I could function. It didn't always work; there were times when the pain nearly blew me apart and I would dash outside, oblivious to the weather, and run as fast as I could to exhaust myself. One time, in the middle of the day, I called a girlfriend to meet me. I left work and sat on a park bench with her to rant and recuperate and get her support until I could go back in and face it all. I found that was the best trick: find your support system, allow yourself to vent, get it out, move on, then focus. It was how I kept my power at work.

Even though I know now that the way a woman dresses doesn't give anyone the right to attack her, in the future, I always wore whatever I had on that day to dinner, like the men did with their daytime business suits. And I coached young women, "Even though it's a fancy restaurant and we're drinking, it's business, so dress that way. You should be able to dress however you want, but that's not the reality."

IN MY DESPERATION and loneliness, and despite the fact that he had maliciously set me up for my doomed dalliance with Bill, I agreed to go out with Greg, who had continued to badger me to date him. My self-talk went like this: *He's a control freak. He has hounded and intimidated me. He's horrible. But there are no other prospects, and I'm so lonely. At least he's single, important, smart, successful, and admired at the company. He has money and wants to spend it on flashy activities. He's a mover and shaker. It will be all right.* I ignored the million alarm bells clanging in my head.

We met for drinks after work, and Greg invited me for a weekend to an elegant lake resort. *Well*, I thought, *that would be exciting. I never get out; I don't have anything going on. I wish I had real friends at work or back in Illinois to do this kind of thing with, but I don't. It's a famous place, and I can't afford this kind of vacation, so it's an opportunity I can't pass up. Why not? I'll do it.*

But then, as we drove along in his sports car through the countryside, Greg barely spoke to me. When he did talk, it was all about Suzanne and her beauty and wit. I tried so hard to be funny and light but ached inside as Greg ignored my attempts at non-Suzanne conversation. Silence—no reaction to any of the things I said. It reminded me too much of my father.

When we got to the lake, we checked in, then immediately jumped into his ski boat, still without exchanging any words. Greg revved up the engine and blasted off, so excessively fast that the boat crashed up and down in the waves, jolting my whole body, leaving spray all over me, but he just cackled and raced around the lake, dismissing my cries of "Stop! Please!"

I clung to the side of the boat so I wouldn't be flung into the cold lake. *Oh my God, is he trying to kill me? Does he hate me for some reason? Am I not funny enough, not interesting enough?*

I'm not Suzanne—is this my punishment? I screamed the whole trip and forced back tears when we finally pulled up to the marina.

That night, I didn't know how to get away, trapped in a hotel room with him. "Well, time for bed," he said, as he stripped naked, grabbed my wrist, and pulled me in. "Let's get it on."

I did it, not because I wanted to, but because of the violence and repercussions I thought might ensue if I didn't. I didn't know how to extricate myself from the situation and followed along passively, trying not to aggravate him until I docked myself securely back in my own house the next day.

I definitely didn't want to go out with Greg anymore and tried to stay away from him. And I never accepted a vacation again just because I wanted to go to an expensive place that I couldn't afford myself—I made sure I really wanted to go with the *person.* There is no free lunch/vacation. But when I tried to avoid Greg, that's when the real harassment started. He would call constantly, during the day and in the middle of the night. Sometimes he would admit that it was he, and sometimes he was just silent on the phone, breathing heavily, like another obscene phone caller. Every time the phone rang, my heart thudded. He wanted to talk about work, then sex, then work, keeping me off balance. I wanted him to leave me alone, but he was my boss's boss—I didn't know what to do.

ONE EVENING I held a routine farm meeting, where I bought supper, as they call dinner in the Midwest, and gave a technical presentation about weed control for a group of local farmers and distributors. Instead of the usual assembly of older, rough-around-the-edges farm types, a young, handsome man with longish dark brown hair and a full mustache to match wandered into the rented hall and sat down next to me. After my slide show, he leaned over and said, "Hi. My name is Alan. Your presentation was really good, very informative. Thanks for all the helpful guidance."

We progressed from there to a rousing conversation, interspersed with our laughter, about corn, fertilizer, and this year's harvest, and I thought, *Wow. Who is this? He's so nice, and he's attractive. And he actually shows interest in my work and what I have to say. He respects me. I can't believe it.*

After the meeting adjourned, he said, "Can I have your phone number? Would it be okay if I called you sometime?"

Even though I thought, *He'll never call. They always say they will, but they don't,* my whole body warmed inside as I glided home, wary but still filled with fantasies of ever after.

The next day, true to his word, Alan called. Our courtship bloomed into dinners cooked together at our homes, lively racquetball matches, good-sport tennis games, and safe jogging together on the street, where no men threw beer cans at me because Alan was by my side. He was from the area, so he invited me one afternoon to drive over and meet his parents, who welcomed me with warmth and home-cooked meals into their close-knit family. His mother and father had been married since they were fifteen and seventeen, respectively, and I envied and admired his secure upbringing, with brother, sister, and relatives nearby. The particular attribute that most drew me to him was that, unlike Ron, he believed me when I told him about Greg's harassment. Alan tried to intervene. He got on the phone when Greg called, told him to stop. But Alan was only twenty-two years old and didn't know how to deal with this middle-aged powermonger.

Greg persevered with his harassment for months. One

night, he called and this time identified himself. He said, "I have to tell you something. I've been checked, and I have VD. Since you and I went out, you probably have it, too."

I crashed the phone into its cradle and slumped into my chair, closing my eyes and running my hands through my hair. I shook my head no, meaning both *No, I can't believe he's haunting me* and *No, I can't have VD from this guy*. I rushed to the hospital for testing, thankful at least that I had been on the pill when I was with him.

The hardest part was my conversation with Alan.

"Alan, I'm totally humiliated, but I have to tell you that I slept with Greg at one point, and now he's saying he has VD, so we both need to get tested. I'm so ashamed and furious and so, so sorry."

"Well, I'm sorry, too, for both of us. We'll just get tested and carry on," Alan said, so generous to me, but I couldn't even look him in the eye for weeks.

About a month later, Greg called and chuckled on the phone, "You know, I never actually had VD. I just wanted to see what you would do."

Anger welled up in me, until I thought I could have actually maimed him if he were there in person. *What a total, complete scumbag*, I thought, *What an unconscionable, evil trick just to retaliate against me and to torment me and Alan.*

I scolded myself, *You should never have gone out with him, Lucinda. You brought this all upon yourself, and now you've hurt Alan. Even though Greg made this whole thing up, maybe it can't be called harassment, because you dated him. That was your big mistake.*

EXHAUSTED FROM ALL this turmoil in my Illinois life, I accepted a promotion back in the home office in Missouri as a product manager to coordinate the research and development of herbicide products across the United States. Alan and I had been dating for about a year and had been readying ourselves for marriage. We decided to move the wedding ahead and relocate together, since Alan's job as an area marketing representative was flexible in its location.

At my going-away party at the office, the local marketing manager, Jerry, said to me, "The only thing I regret about your leaving is that I never got to sleep with you."

Ick! He was married, with two kids, and disgusting. As if! Just thinking about him today makes my skin crawl. Anita Hill calls this type of male disease "erotomonomania" and defines it in her book *Speaking Truth to Power* as "a male delusion that attractive young women are harboring fantasies about them." [2] Yep, that nails Jerry.

ALAN AND I loaded up our car and old pea-green truck and caravanned off, each with a dog in the front seat beside us, newlyweds on our fresh adventure. *My career is taking off*, I thought, *and I'm happily married and safe. Life is so good.* The company reimbursed me for my house in Decatur, and, with that money in hand, Alan and I bought our first home together. We put down roots as we arranged our cheap, first-time furniture and home-goods wedding presents around the rooms. When I unpacked my books and reports onto the shelves of my new office cubicle, I vowed to stay as far away from Greg as possible. I assumed marriage would protect me from further gender-based mistreatment and harassment, but I found out that wasn't a true hypothesis.

About six months later, on one business trip to Kansas with two male coworkers, I began feeling weak and shaky but chalked it up to the fact that I was three months pregnant at the time. I didn't mention it to my colleagues, since I hadn't told anyone at work about my pregnancy, fearing the repercussions. I slogged through that day of farm visits in hot and dusty sorghum fields, clumping around in heavy steel-toed boots. When I finally got back to the hotel, I collapsed in bed early, only to wake up in the middle of the night with intense abdominal spasms. In the bathroom, I saw blood in the toilet and knew something was wrong. Cramping and doubling over, I placed a long-distance call, as we had to do in those days, to the hospital back home. A competent RN informed me how to watch for bleeding, saying, "Sometimes that's normal in the first few months, honey. It's okay."

I suffered on through the night, until one episode in the bathroom resulted in chunks of tissue along with the blood. I called the nurse again, and she said I might be having a miscarriage. "Just hang in there, sweetie," she said.

More fragments, more blood. It went on all night while I watched *Caddyshack*, the only movie on at three in the morning. The one scene I remember is with the Baby Ruth in the pool, which I didn't find at all funny at the time. I talked to Alan multiple times on the phone, crying and panicky and deeply alone.

By morning, I knew I had lost my baby. I had cried all night over the reality of it, the fact that I wasn't going to have a baby after all. It was gone, just like that, after all the joy and excitement. The next morning, I managed to make it to the hotel lobby, stumbling and dragging my suitcase, where I bumped into my colleagues. "I've had a miscarriage," I in-

formed them. They were married men with children, so I figured they would understand.

But they both turned away immediately, faces twisted and
noses wrinkled, and, without a word, scurried off to the waiting taxi. I struggled to get in while they continued an animated
conversation about work, ignoring me completely. When we
got to the airport, they ditched me. I didn't see them again
until I boarded the plane, where they sat side by side, turning
their crisp-cut identical heads away from me as they kept up
their business debate. Thank God for a sympathetic flight attendant who asked, "What's wrong, dear?" and responded with
kindness, a pillow, and water when I told her, "Last night I had
a miscarriage in my hotel room on a business trip."

To this day, it's hard for me to understand the men's reaction. Were they thinking, *This is why women don't belong in the
workplace*, or were they just so uncomfortable that they
couldn't even try to deal with me?

I got a similar non-response when I called the office after
my plane landed. I told the secretary and my boss, "I just got
back from Kansas this morning, but I'm afraid I won't be in
this afternoon, because I was pregnant and I had a miscarriage
last night."

My manager said, "Oh, uh, okay."

Thankfully, his secretary, Diane, responded with human
warmth. She helped me find a doctor and get an appointment
to have a D and C. I cherished her acts of kindness, just like
the flight attendant's. No one mentioned it at work the next
day, when I returned to the office. I vowed that, in the workplace, I would never ignore or discount any tragedy of a colleague, boss, or employee—including death, miscarriage, loss
of a child, and so on. In my mind, it's cowardly just to scuttle
away and pretend nothing has happened. Especially when it

came to pregnancy and birth, because of my personal experience, I spoke up to both the fathers and the mothers with whom I worked. It irked me that pregnancy was treated as a disability under the law, but that's how most people saw it—something was wrong with you, and it was somehow repellent. I showed small acts of kindness to expecting parents whenever I could. I always inquired after both my male and female colleagues and employees, "How is the pregnancy going? I hope you're going to take some time off. I took only six weeks off with my first child because I thought I had to prove I was a hard worker. Don't do that! The work will always be there. Take this special time with your baby."

If things went well, my employees and I celebrated with baby showers for both fathers and mothers, and I supported their parental leave. If things went awry, I offered sympathy and empathy, based on my own struggles, to the parents and didn't just sweep tragedies under the office rug. My employees and colleagues wanted to talk about these things and always responded, "Lucinda, thank you so much for asking. Yes, we had a miscarriage, but we're working through it. Thanks for sharing your own experiences with us. We appreciate being able to talk about it with you." It takes bravery to be kind in the face of hardship—and we all should be brave, just like the flight attendant and the secretary who supported me.

SINCE I WAS back in the home office again, every day I observed Greg's higher-up, Dr. Tim Johnson, the vice president of research and product development. Like Greg, Tim also liked to hold court around the coffeepot. Just hearing his voice booming across the cubicle jungle made me shudder. I had witnessed what he could do to someone he didn't like. There was a Filipino man, Dr. Christian Ocampo, one of only two nonwhite members in our group. Christian was a nice guy, funny and smart, and I liked him. Then Tim started telling all his employees that Christian was a persona non grata and that we shouldn't eat lunch with him. It was never clear what he had done to earn this disrespect, besides the obvious racism on Tim's part. But no one seemed to need any facts.

Pretty soon, everyone was avoiding Christian. One day after a week or so of this gossip from Tim, I saw him sitting alone in the cafeteria. I gripped my tray, strode toward him, and plopped down in the empty seat beside him. I will never forget his look of gratitude, especially because it was my last chance to show him direct compassion and solidarity. The following day, either because Tim fired him or because he quit, Christian was gone.

Next came a black man, Dr. Ned Jackson, who had top credentials from a prestigious university. Tim started rumors about him, too, saying he was incompetent, and used the same freeze-out tactic, telling everyone not to associate with him. Ned had little field experience and asked multiple colleagues to allow him to accompany them so he could grasp the real crop world. No one would do it, because of Ned's ostracized status. When I invited him to come with me, furious warnings erupted: "You can't travel with a black man" and "A black man and a white woman working together is repulsive."

Ned's last name was the same as mine—Jackson. This led to further outcry: "Everyone will think you're married." Ned and I went on a successful trip, with no problems, but shortly after that, he, too, was gone from the company.

I figured I was next in the "women and minorities" category, so I tried to avoid Tim whenever I could and just lie low. But it didn't work; I was in his crosshairs.

On a business trip to New York one night, I told the other employees with me that I was going into the city to see an old college friend and go ice-skating with him in Central Park. When I got back to the office the next week, Tim had spread rumors that I was having an affair with a man in New York, and that I was using business hours for a sordid rendezvous. The technique was the same that Lonnie used against me in Northern California—to "ruin" me so that I would quit in shame.

Alan accompanied me to the office in my defense. We had an appointment with Tim to elucidate the truth, but each time we tried to approach him, his secretary intervened. She said he was on the phone, late for a meeting, gone for the day, even though we could see him slinking in and out of his office. She pawned us off on Tim's right-hand man, Dr. Frank Simmons, who wiggled around in his chair, hemming and hawing. Fidgeting, his eyes all over the room, he made it obvious that he knew Tim was lying but also that, afraid for his job, he wouldn't do anything. Frank had his whole career ahead of him; he wouldn't touch this mess.

A few weeks later, Tim made a pronouncement: "No one in my shop without a PhD will ever be promoted. It's a new requirement. If you don't have a PhD, you aren't qualified to do higher-level jobs in this group."

Since I was the only one there without a PhD, it was obvious that I was the one under attack. He couldn't directly fire me, but he was determined to find a way to make me leave. I decided to go back to school and get a PhD. It was an ugly way to exit, but I had learned a thing or two by then and was able to finagle a scholarship from the company for my graduate work at a local university.

The gold nugget in the wreckage was that I got the corporation to pay for my PhD, with no obligation to return to work there. I admit it was a small act of revenge. But since I didn't know how to sue them for all the bullying they'd put me through, I figured out another way to make them pay, literally, by proposing a research project on one of their products that would bring them results and academic buy-in. They approved it, and I got funding for my schooling and my project, with enough money left over to buy supplies and hire a (female) research assistant.

I reported Greg to Human Resources when I left the company—but only after sleepless nights of fear about speaking out. Multiple times, I headed to the door of the HR representative in a sweat, only to turn around and creep to the bathroom instead. Finally, shaking and with an enormous rock in my stomach, I walked in, sat down in the guest chair in front of her desk, and told her about it. I confessed that I was bringing this up only because I was leaving, and that I would never have said a word if I had still been working there; I'd have been too afraid of the repercussions: getting fired, getting blackballed, getting harassed even more than I already was.

She didn't even flinch when I told her about Greg. In fact, she said, "You know, we've had almost ten complaints about him. If this happens one more time, we're going to have to do something about it."

So, Greg wasn't just harassing Suzanne and me—he was a master at it. But there was no female camaraderie in the company at that time. The HR representative was probably as afraid as I was about damaging her career. We women were there only because they "let" us be there. We were told we weren't really qualified and that a man could replace us in a minute, and we believed it.

I crawled from the office after all my angst, all my trials in getting up my nerve to report Greg. All that and then no real reaction, no consequences for him—nothing.

I HAD BEEN rolling the PhD thing over in my mind for some time. Tim's threats and shenanigans, plus the aftershocks of trying to report Greg's harassment, were the final punches I needed to return to academia. That, along with Alan's pointed advice "Either go get your PhD or stop talking about it," pushed me over the edge. I hoped the university environment would be a kinder, gentler world than the corporate one I was leaving. But I quickly found that a change in venue didn't eliminate sexual harassment.

LEGAL AND SOCIAL CHANGE TAKES ROOT

CORPORATIONS STRUGGLED IN the late '70s with the new concept of equality of women in the workplace. President Lyndon B. Johnson added "sex" to the antidiscrimination list for affirmative action in 1967. Up until then, discrimination in hiring and employment had been illegal only on the basis of race, color, religion, or national origin. Johnson's Executive Order 11375 was applied in the early '70s to government agencies and universities, but large corporations fought the order on into the late 1970s, when then-president Jimmy Carter's administration began using the order against them. Companies dragged their feet but realized that new laws now prevented discrimination against women in the workplace and that they were going to have to do something to get with the times.

During this period, I spent a lot of time wondering, *Why*

am I harassed so much in these male-dominated jobs? It's even worse than when I was a waitress. It doesn't make any sense, because I'm not sexy or particularly feminine. I'm not a tomboy, but I'm no glamour queen or Miss America contender.

Years later, a 2007 study finally clarified for me that sexual harassment is motivated not by sexual desire, as we know, but rather by "a desire to punish gender-role deviants and, therefore, is directed at women who violate feminine ideals." Women in the study who violated feminine ideals had relatively masculine personalities (e.g., assertive, dominant, and independent) and experienced the most sexual harassment. And women in male-dominated organizations were harassed more than women in female-dominated organizations. Women in male-dominated organizations who had relatively masculine personalities were sexually harassed the most. [3]

Now I got it. I exhibited independent, competitive qualities in a male-dominated company. The men didn't like it, saw me as a deviant, and wanted to punish me. And I guess I did that—upended feminine ideals. At our off-site corporate meetings, there were usually options for the afternoon recreation activities, and I always chose one of the "men's" events, like golf, tennis, or river rafting, because I liked the outdoors and the action. When I played tennis at these outings, I would win—and I see now that the men didn't like it, just as my father had warned me. I wanted promotions and a career, and that didn't jibe with how men thought women should act.

Laws and customs around sexual harassment continued to evolve during the late 1970s. Under Title VII in 1976, the first federal court recognized sexual harassment as sexual discrimination. The US court of appeals reversed the 1974 case *Barnes v. Train*, and it ruled in 1977 that a manager retaliating against a female employee for rejecting his sexual advances was indeed committing sexual harassment and breaching Title VII.

But legal progress was slow. Women had to almost suffer a nervous breakdown to demonstrate that harassment affected them. This standard was upheld even as late as 1986, in the Supreme Court case of *Rabidue v. Osceola Refining Company*. The court characterized Vivienne Rabidue as strong, capable, and ambitious, and concluded that the sexual harassment she experienced was therefore not truly damaging. The prevailing view put the onus back on the victim. If the victim weathered the storm, didn't fall apart, and went on with her work, the harassment must not have been that bad. Women like me experienced sleepless nights and high anxiety, but if we plugged away, we were penalized.

Retaliation like the kind Lonnie and Greg dished out to me was legal in the 1970s. It wasn't considered harassment; you had to be fired to get anyone's attention, and even that was questionable, as I found out when Mr. Don fired me from my waitress job. It was 2006 before a landmark anti-retaliation claim finally came to the Supreme Court after nine years of legal wrangling. In *Burlington Northern & Santa Fe Railway Company v. White*, Sheila White, a forklift operator, sued her company for demoting and suspending her without pay after she complained about sexual harassment from her immediate supervisor. She finally won her case, and that became a precedent that an action other than full dismissal from a job could be considered an "adverse employment act." But back in the '70s, what Lonnie and Greg had done was not considered retaliatory or anything all that bad.

My self-admonition that I couldn't say Greg harassed me because I had dated him was valid, and I wasn't the only one baffled about it. For years, the courts grappled with "date rape"—when a person is raped by someone she knows, like a boyfriend, or anyone with whom she may have had a romantic or potentially sexual relationship. Laws tended to justify date rape and blame victims for sexual assault by pointing to the existence of a previous romantic relationship. It was not considered a crime in America to assault a former girlfriend or wife until the first state, South Dakota, declared it illegal in 1975. It took almost twenty years for the rest of the states to come to the same conclusion. This belief that post-relationship sexual affronts were not a crime extended to sexual harassment. The sexual assault or harassment was considered consensual if there had been an intimate relationship prior to the harassment, so no action could be taken against the assailant.

Date rape and post-relationship harassment were better defined in the 1980s and '90s, but they're still controversial today. Now, at least, it's fairly accepted that just because we dated a man, it doesn't give him the right to harass us. Many companies try to protect themselves against this situation and potential sexual harassment liability by requiring dating and relationship agreements. If coworkers are involved with each other romantically, they are supposed to disclose that the relationship is voluntary so that a supervisor can document it, change supervisor-subordinate reporting, if necessary, and provide expectations for proper workplace conduct. These agreements include language such as "We will inform the company immediately if the relationship ends, or if the conduct or advances of the other person are no longer welcome. We agree that if the relationship ends, we will respect the other person's decision to end the relationship and not pursue that person or seek to resume the relationship or engage in any other conduct towards the other person that could violate the Harassment-Free Workplace Policy." [4]

Decades later, when I was a manager, I enforced these

agreements a few times. But I'd never seen them before 2010. They were certainly not around when Greg was torturing me post breakup.

We were all intimidated by the news we read that a woman could be dragged by her hair through a dirty ditch over her former sexual encounters and that her past could be used against her in court—so it was a scary proposition even to think about legal action. This situation in the late '70s would not change for twenty years.

Sexual harassment was coming out in the news when *The New York Times* first used the phrase in the summer of 1975. [5] A *Redbook* survey in 1976 revealed that 92 percent of women said sexual harassment was a problem at work, and nearly 50 percent said that they had been fired or quit their job because of it. [6] Research showed that eighteen million women in America were sexually harassed at work in 1979 and 1980. [7]

Along with Helen Gurley Brown in the 1960s, we still had our antifeminist women. In the late 1970s, Phyllis Schlafly perpetuated the belief that women "asked for it," in regard to rape and sexual harassment, and said, in 1981, "Sexual harassment on the job is not a problem for the virtuous woman." [8]

At this stage in my own career, I felt the shift from sexual harassment in traditional women's jobs, where the men wanted to "keep me down," to the harassment I now faced in men's jobs, where they wanted to "keep me out." I didn't know what was causing this shift, but now I see that they just really wanted me to go away. I didn't realize how much men wanted their world to stay their own. My very presence was the problem.

In those years, men were largely successful at keeping us out of science and technical fields. If we got in, they drove us to quit through an unwelcoming and sexually harassing atmosphere. Many of the prejudices that existed in the 1970s remain intact decades later in science, technology, and engineering companies and keep the number of women in these professions low. In 2018, women made up only 28 percent of the science and engineering workforce nationwide, according to the National Science Foundation. [9] Of Google's technical workforce in 2017, only 20 percent of its current employees and 21 percent of its new hires are women. [10]

five

UPPING THE GAME

I THOUGHT I HAD IT ALL FIGURED OUT. I WAS MARRIED, planning to become pregnant again, and on my way to getting my PhD. I knew from my miscarriage experience (and everything else) that corporate America was a hostile place to have a baby, so my strategy was to get pregnant in graduate school. I found out later there was a Pregnancy Discrimination Act, enacted in 1978, that said employers couldn't discriminate on the basis of pregnancy, but it didn't do me any good in 1981. No one told me about this new law, and it certainly wasn't brought up in the workplace. On the contrary, I knew my managers and colleagues would discriminate against me if I were pregnant while working. I could be subject to ill treatment, maybe suffer a demotion, and possibly lose my job. With my corporate funding in hand, I applied to graduate school in a college town in nearby Illinois so Alan could keep his company position and I could have a baby. Plus, I figured once I had a PhD, nobody could say I wasn't qualified anymore. I'd get all the credentials; I'd smash another obstacle that men put in my way; I'd play their game.

By this time, I knew that men were not my friends. Every male professor, boss, colleague, and man on the street was suspect, and I regarded each one warily, thinking, *What is he going to try to get from me? How is he going to use me?* And, back in the academic setting, there were more field trips and conferences—real opportunities for men to prey on me. One of my two major professors, Dr. Lewis Landers, constantly bothered me with offers to get a drink, just the two of us, to visit the research field station together for the weekend, to share a quiet dinner, or to have a nice chat in his office. I burned or hid all the notes, cards, and presents he sent me, fearful that I'd be accused of "putting out" in order to gain his favoritism, knowing it would all reflect back on me, not him—that his attention would be construed as my fault, not his. On the weekends, he would call me from the field station, where he hunkered down to get away from his wife. I knew he had been drinking as he slurred his words, mixing sexual desire and work requests: "I wish you were here with me. No one else is around. There's a cot here we could sleep on. We could have fun together. Can you come next weekend? You could work on your split-plot field design. You need to get that finished soon, you know. You'd better come."

I spent my PhD years fighting him off, thinking up excuses, avoiding being alone with him—all factors that robbed me of focus and time on my research, my scientific goals, my career, my life.

One evening, he and his wife invited me and my mother, who was visiting me, over for dinner. He stared at me the whole night. My mother joked about it, "I think Dr. Landers has a fatherly crush on you. It's so cute." But it wasn't funny. I couldn't tell her he was making me miserable, that it was a constant strain, that it was affecting my work. I knew how she always regarded everything as the woman's fault, so I didn't want to go there. She still saw men's attention, even unwanted, as a generous tribute from a man to a woman. I knew I couldn't explain the humiliation to her or the impact it was having on me. Plus, women of her generation were masters at putting up with it, taking it as a sick compliment—it was their way of coping.

As part of my graduate research, I worked with other agriculturalists and weed scientists around Illinois, where I had my field research trials. As results came in, I presented papers at various conferences to share my findings. As much as I enjoyed public speaking and the opportunity to have my research exhibited and reviewed by my colleagues, these gatherings were still sexist and exhausting.

At multiple major professional weed science conferences, Dr. Ray Gillen, a famous professor at one Midwest university, was a featured speaker on agronomic crops. Thumbs tucked under his red suspenders, he would cry in his good-old-boy Oklahoma accent, "Hey, look at those tomatoes!" as he used his pointer to emphasize the large tomatoes in place of the breasts of a naked woman on his slide. I'd seen it many times, but to him, it never got old.

It didn't get old, either, to the 99-percent-male audience, who thought this was original and hilarious. As the next speaker, another well-known academic, showed a photo of a nude woman with a hoe on a tractor and said, "Whoops! How did that get in there?" they all fell apart hee-hawing.

Inserting a "surprise" naked-woman picture in a boring slide presentation was a common tactic to perk up the men, causing them all to cheer and start paying attention again. We few women gritted our teeth. There we were with our polite smiles, trying to be part of the gang, while the men looked at us to gauge our reaction. I never wanted them to see me sweat, so I would simper and fake-laugh. The parallel-universe Lucinda rebelled inside her head, furious and wanting to sock them in their big stomachs.

WHEN I GOT pregnant on schedule, I told my major professors that they didn't have to worry; I wouldn't miss any work at all. I would have the baby between when summer school ended (late August) and fall semester started (early September) and be right back at it.

For my medical care, I went to the local hospital to a well-known, recommended ob-gyn who had been in town for decades. Alan accompanied me for the first few visits; then it got repetitive and it was hard for him to miss work, so, at around five months pregnant, I opted to go alone to my appointments. Stripped naked under my little hospital gown, I waited for my doctor in his examining room. He entered with the usual pleasantries: "How are you today? How is everything going?" But as I sat up on the tissue-papered table, he began stroking my leg and touching me on the inside of my thigh.

Even though I got that heart-in-the-throat feeling, I was hopeful: *That was just an accident. He didn't mean to do that; he was just adjusting the sheet or something.*

Then it happened again, and then again, more aggressively, with leg rubbing and flicks at my crotch for my seven-month checkup, and I knew it wasn't any accident. *Is nothing sacred? Here I am, seven months pregnant, and I thought all this was behind me. I'm a married woman with a child coming. Not this again.* I called several doctors and tried to switch, but no one would take me.

They all said, "He's a fine doctor; there's no reason to switch at this late point in your pregnancy," even though I alluded to my desperation.

Finally, I became bolder and told one of the young doctors that his colleague was harassing me. I started to cry and said, "That's why I have to switch doctors."

He went quiet on the phone. Then, after a long pause, he said, "I'll take you. But we will never talk about this again."

I hung up and heaved a long shudder. *He believed me*, I thought. Tears spewed from the corners of my eyes, releasing a fraction of my pent-up anxiety. But I understood that my new doctor was going to protect his colleague with his silence. This behavior kept it all under wraps during that era, as it still does today.

Of course, nothing was done about the offending doctor. I didn't report him to anyone else, and my new doctor didn't do anything about the harassment. The guy went on practicing and harassing other pregnant women and young girls, I'm sure. I didn't have it in me to stop him, though I would love to have the chance now. But back then, I just wanted to disentangle from him, to save myself. Sadly, I didn't have the knowledge or the confidence to try to save others. That would come later.

MY AMAZING SON Dane was born two months later, and I charged into motherhood, graduate school, and my new teaching and graduate assistant jobs. The professors and students in the Child Development department at my university ran a five-star infant care center on campus. As part of their "study" of him, they reviewed full notes on every moment of my son's day with me each evening. I rode my bicycle to school with Dane in his bike seat, dropped him off at the infant center, attended class or worked in the lab, then stopped by every couple of hours to nurse and play with him.

When I got married and had a child, I thought I could stow away my lifetime of harassment and programming to be subservient to men into some inaccessible corner and just move forward with my new life. But I held on to reams of anger about my perception of men's power over me. I began realizing how years of sexual harassment had messed up sex for me, as it had so long been used against me as a power play. I found myself all caught up in who had the upper hand, instead of actually enjoying it. I performed like a machine, focused on getting attention, not really into it for me or for him. And I acted like I didn't care—impersonating a man by getting up first before he could reject me and get up himself. I pretended to be busy, said I had to go, as if I had the power.

Questions about my past still gnawed at me: *Was the sexual harassment my fault? Did I give off a vulnerable vibe because of my neediness? Did that encourage men to go after me? Did I want power in sex because it was a way of getting back at those who used my gender and sexuality against me?* My insecure self still wanted to take the blame. But then another, stronger side of me would kick in and think, *I want to be kinder to my earlier self. It wasn't my fault. I never "asked for it." I never said, "Please attack me and make me uncomfortable and demean me professionally." No, never.*

I envisioned different expectations for women that hadn't yet reached the central United States. I wanted an equal partnership in marriage and parenthood, and I wasn't getting it. I didn't blend into the time-honored male-female roles of the Midwest, where the woman wrestles with the housework and child raising and the man holds down his job. Alan, as a local Illinoisan, comfortably embraced a traditional division of labor. His father asked him to go hunting in Montana the same week Dane was due to be born, and Alan accepted the invitation. When I found out, I said, "How can you possibly leave me? How can you even think about missing the most important event in our lives? I can't believe you."

His father's response was "Women have been having babies alone forever—what's the big deal? What kind of man lets his wife tell him what to do?"

After arguing and trying to please both father and wife, Alan declined the hunting expedition, but it left me with a sour ball in my mouth that I couldn't choke down.

I had all these reflections and questions but not many answers. This pattern, of course, affected my marriage, which wasn't going well.

THINGS CAME TO a head for me in 1982. In addition to fighting off harassment from my major professor, I shouldered a full graduate school course load, a job teaching college-level statistics, an unfinished thesis, a four-month-old baby, a non-participatory husband, two dogs, and two cats. And I had no family around for support. I had said yes to everything for a long time and strove to live up to being Connie Ann, my mother's nickname for me in the 1950s, because I was conscientious and always did my best. I studied hard, kept up those straight A's, catered to Alan's hunting and boating passions, provided complete love and care to my child every moment possible, and brought in a decent salary. I had said yes to the dogs because Alan wanted them, yes to the cats because they needed homes, yes to Alan's participation in sports because I wanted to be a supportive wife, yes to all the housework and childcare because I wanted to be a good homemaker and mother. It turns out that by saying yes to Alan's rugby, basketball, and softball, I allowed him to say no to fatherhood. I agreed to sit in the bleachers night after night, holding Dane late into the evening, so that Alan could play out on the court or the field like the other guys on the team who had that wife and that baby watching and cheering them on. I didn't fit in with the other moms, who were younger, didn't work, and were not in school. As I sat there with my crying, hungry baby in a dirty diaper, who should have been home in his crib, I pictured arriving late for work the next day and failing my eight o'clock exam. But we had only one car, and I worried that if I left early, Alan would feel deserted and think I was a bad wife. I stayed and fumed inside for each long game, which always had extra innings or overtime.

I didn't complain when our dog Ox repeatedly dug a hole under the fence and encouraged Yogi, his small Sheltie sidekick, to escape. Galloping after them, I'd see their little faces out the back window of the dogcatcher's van and know we were in for another fifty dollar fine that was way past our budget. When Ox felled the only tree in the backyard, I dealt with the landlord and didn't insist we get rid of the dogs.

It was all becoming physically impossible. One person can be only so many places at one time (one, actually). But I kept myself busy, busy, busy while I avoided dealing with the things in my past that haunted me. I had played in a tennis tournament when I was eight months pregnant and berated myself when I lost in the finals. *How could you have lost, Lucinda? You didn't run fast enough for the last shot. You let her ace you in the last set. You're a failure—you should have won!* An advanced aerobics class and nine holes of golf were standard fare the day I gave birth. I pedaled furiously from home to school to childcare during the day and was up most nights studying for exams, cleaning the house, doing laundry, nursing, and caring for Dane. My silent accommodation of everyone left me seething inside, and I knew I had to get off the whirring conveyor belt. Leaving my marriage was one alternative.

In the middle of all this doubt and self-analysis, I neared the end of my PhD program. Finally, the day came when I nervously entered the small, stuffy conference room to face five men and defend my dissertation. I'd finished all my coursework, my thesis, and my written exams, and now only this oral defense remained. I was going to be Dr. Jackson! I could taste it. I was ready. I knew my stuff. Bring on the questions!

But instead of fielding questions about the results of my research, my contributions to science, or why plant physiology was important to the world, the first thing I heard was, "Why are you wearing what you're wearing today? What was your thought process in choosing your outfit? You look pretty, by the way."

What was this? That familiar sinking feeling came over me, clouding my brain and throwing me off my game. *Am I not here because of my work? Isn't that what we're supposed to talk about? What do my clothes, my looks, have to do with this? Would these people ask a man that question?*

In defense of their harassment and unwanted comments, men always say, "Gosh, I can't even compliment a woman anymore." But they know the difference. Compliments make us feel good; harassment makes us feel degraded. So, yeah, go ahead and give a compliment, but don't sexualize it. And how about complimenting that woman on her finesse in negotiating a good deal, managing a thorny project snafu, or completing her thesis? There are other types of compliments besides appearance-based ones.

I expect that men were confused then, too. I know they didn't all have malicious intent. My PhD committee members were perhaps thinking that they were *supposed* to compliment a woman on her physical image. They often didn't know what to say to women, and tripped over saying "girls" versus "women" and "Ms." versus "Miss." One reason I wanted to get a PhD was so I would stop getting the annoying question "Is it Mrs. or Miss? Or are you one of those women's-libber 'Ms.' types?"

With my new degree, I could say simply, "It's Dr. Jackson, thank you very much."

But some of the men were just purposely slow to learn. Maybe they were bewildered, but they used their confusion as an excuse for continued sexism. And it didn't help at my PhD orals that the question about my wardrobe came from Dr. Landers, the professor who had been harassing me. It's too bad that the other men in the room didn't speak up to help me by saying something like, "Well, that's not an appropriate question; let's move on." Even if it made some of them uncomfortable, they didn't do anything to stop it. At the end of the session, while my committee deliberated, I paced outside the room in the beige pantsuit I thought made me look professional, not pretty. They emerged smiling, giving me handshakes all around. "Congratulations, Dr. Jackson! Congratulations, Dr. Jackson!" Even though I still bristled over the clothing curveball they'd thrown at me, my heart soared.

Still, that one triumph wasn't enough to offset the heaviness that all my other obligations caused. Writing down everything that overextended me or caused me to feel like a second-class citizen, I scrolled through my list. I wound down my statistics instructor position and didn't volunteer to teach another class—check. I wrapped up the final details of my doctorate in record time—check. The only nonnegotiable item, the one thing that definitely was staying, was Baby Dane. Everything else was expendable, in jeopardy, as I picked off one entry after the next. I backed off on the housework and let the house be a little dirty—check. I sent all the dogs and cats off to good homes—check. I quit punching the clock in the bleachers of my husband's sports events—check. As for Alan, I gave him one last chance by setting up couples' counseling for us, threatening divorce if he didn't attend—check.

When negotiations and counseling didn't improve my relationship with Alan or my requested division of our labor, I spoke with a lawyer at the university and told Alan I was filing for divorce. His response was similar—just substitute "I" pronouns for "he" pronouns—to what his mother said to me on the phone when she heard the news: "What's wrong with you? He's a great husband. He doesn't beat you, does he? He doesn't run with other women, right? He doesn't come home drunk. What's the problem?"

It was hard to explain the husband-wife responsibility sharing that I craved, but my insides were empty and I couldn't smile at Alan anymore. As I soapboxed on about communication, I felt like I was hitting him over the head with his own softball bat. My ranting should have caused a skull fracture, but it didn't even daze him. I couldn't get his attention, even though he later conceded, "I know that my past has not prepared me for the type of communication required for a good relationship—friendship or marriage."

I don't recommend that you wait until you snap to take charge of your life. Do it now, before you get to that point. But just so I don't make it sound too simple, let me tell you that this undoing and moving forward took almost two years. For me, the long process of growing my self-esteem, becoming a mother, and earning my PhD helped me make the change. I'd had small baby steps and revelations along the way, like the motel maid who told me not to kneel down for anyone, and the protest at Roy Rogers where we got the harasser fired. I don't believe in one "trigger" moment that often features in a best seller—one pivotal event that changes everything. It makes for a good read, but it's not real life, in my experience.

Real life is a series of slow, small, iterative events that result in gradual change and self-awareness. And it's combined with a lot of steps backward along the way. So don't feel bad if you don't have one key "aha" moment when everything changes for the better. It's all right that it takes a while and is sometimes so slow that you don't even see it or know it's happening.

Motherhood was a factor for me—I had someone now whom I loved more than anything in the world, and I wanted the best for him. I thought, *I never want anyone to bully Dane, so why am I letting people bully me? I want to be a role model for him. I want him to be proud of me as he grows up.*

Earning a PhD was also instrumental in my change from victim to survivor. It took away some of the doubt men had instilled in me about my abilities, some of the accusations that a woman couldn't do the job. Now I had a diploma that many men didn't have, and it would be harder for them to discount me.

I knew that getting back to California would be good for me, too. In my old home base, there were people who knew me, like my sister, Deborah, my longtime friend Linda, and old friends from college. Their support showed me the wisdom of not trying to do everything alone. I was learning how to use my network and resources and not be ashamed to admit I needed help.

I WAS A divorced, single mother with a one-year-old baby and I needed a job. But I was thirty-two years old now and armed with my PhD, and I had five years of corporate experience on my résumé, so I headed with hope into the arduous process of job searching and interviews.

One role particularly intrigued me. It was a research position with a big chemical company that operated all over the world. It was headquartered in the Midwest, but its research laboratories were in California. The job was leading one of their herbicide groups to design and invent herbicides that were effective and safe to humans and the environment. It was a solid fit for me. I flew out there for the interview.

It didn't start well. As I huddled with the prospective group leader, Jack, in his cramped and smoky office, he said, "I don't think I should hire you. Because you're divorced, you must not be reliable. You don't have commitment, and it's risky to bring you onboard."

My heart sank. These were the days when men could say anything they wanted in an interview. My sister had just had an interview where they'd asked her, "Are you on birth control? What type of birth control? We don't want you getting pregnant. You women just get pregnant and leave."

But I was older and stronger now. I stared into Jack's tired old face as he lit another cigarette, and I said, "That's just not fair." Then I outlined all the ways in which I'd shown tenacity and professionalism in my career.

I got the job. I moved to California, Dane in tow. And, for the first time, I made a career choice that wasn't based on a man.

I'd been in my new position for a few months when a recent hire, Craig, joined our research group. On Craig's first day at the lab, his boss, Will, brought him into the cafeteria to have lunch and meet some of his new workmates.

As I sat at a full table with my colleagues, Will spotted me and said, "Lucinda, this is Craig. He's single, like you, so you two should get married and have babies."

I rolled my eyes toward the ceiling and felt my face flush. I wanted to welcome our new coworker and make a good impression, but, with my newfound attitude, I looked Will right in the face and said, "Well, that would be just great. And we'll name our firstborn Will, after you."

That really shut him up. He turned purple and tiptoed away.

Luckily for me, when I worked in California at the lab during the '80s, sexual harassment took more of a backseat than it had in the pandemic '70s. There was some awareness of it now, and new laws against it. There was another woman manager besides me—a first. Finally, I wasn't the only woman in the room or the bean field. Harassment hadn't totally worked for men—there were now women in the workplace in men's jobs. They hadn't prevented us from getting in, and some of us had persisted. I could hear the men around me as if they said it out loud, "If we have to have women around, let's at least keep them in low-level positions." A few of us got in, but could we get ahead?

Until recently, I presumed that the waning of sexual harassment at that time had to do with my age—that I had become "unfuckable," as Amy Schumer has said. [1] Women often believe this, and our youth culture leads us to actually feel remorseful about it—"I'm not harassed anymore because I'm old and wrinkled." A poll investigating sexual harassment at different age ranges showed that 56 percent of women, the highest number, experienced workplace sexual harassment at ages eighteen to thirty-four, reinforcing my beliefs that you had to be young to be harassed. But the poll also revealed that 44 percent of women ages thirty-five to forty-nine and 41 percent of women at fifty-plus years old still reported harassment at work. [2] Sexual harassment might taper off, but it's not over as you get older.

Even though, as I approached my forties, I finally had some power, my womanhood was a continual obstacle to my career ambitions. My big dream was that Dane and I would move to Hong Kong on an international assignment. Plenty of men were relocating internationally for the company at that time, and I saw it as a perfect opportunity for me. I would make more money, it would be a boon to my career to have global experience under my belt, and I could find inexpensive full-time nanny care there. Hong Kong was modern and sophisticated; I had checked all this out on business trips to Asia. When a position opened up there, I applied for it and was immediately told there were no international assignments for women—because women didn't belong overseas.

When I asked why, my managers quickly rebuffed me with all kinds of patronizing, illogical reasons: "It's not safe, and businessmen there wouldn't accept you. Single women can't do these jobs anyway; it's best for you to stay in the United States, since you have a child."

For years, I had traveled all over the world and been well received by working men in Asia, South America, Africa, Europe, and the Middle East. The major problems I had were solely with male managers and colleagues within my own companies. An international assignment was a prerequisite to higher-level positions; I knew I would be good at it, but I was never going to get one.

The company informed us in 1988 that it had decided to close its California facilities and move all the employees either to the world headquarters or to a new research facility in the Midwest. I had a choice to make. Part of me was willing to go back to the Midwest for a promotion. The other part of me saw the past Lucinda jumping up and down, waving a big STAY BACK banner, reminding me that I'd struggled there without support from family and friends. And I had just started dating Craig—coincidentally, the colleague Will had said I should marry and have babies with six years before. Craig had jumped ship early and quit, joining a big oil, gas, and energy company located in California. So, once again debating with myself, I asked, *Should I follow opportunities for my career or follow a man?*

Fortunately, I had come to see that there were other options and that maybe it didn't have to be one or the other. I interviewed for and received an offer as a manager in the Agricultural Chemical division at the same Fortune 500 company where Craig worked. It was a step up and more money, a greater number of employees to supervise, and more responsibility. And it was in California, where Craig was.

Craig and I grew closer as we camped, hiked, and explored museums around the Bay Area—activities that seamlessly included Dane. Though many men balk at dating women with children, Craig told me, "Dane's a positive. He's such a sensitive and smart child. Not only can I see that you're an accomplished career person, but I especially admire the responsible and loving mother you are."

I fell in love when Dane had a breakdown at Disneyland and Craig put his arms around my son and soothed him back to normalcy. We had animated conversations about science, life, our pasts, our futures. I loved driving to his parents' house, where they embraced Dane with special food and activities suited to a seven-year-old. We all sat around the table, engaged in lively, comfortable conversations. Craig and I shared similar views on money, religion, politics, education, child rearing, and love. Despite our shared past marriage failures, we both wanted to give the institution another chance. Six years of singlehood and single motherhood had been good for me. I had a stronger sense of self and made better decisions on my own. I resolved that I would take the job and marry Craig.

This time, I chose my path based on a job *and* on a man with whom I had a real future, realizing that you *can* have both.

However, as before with Alan, getting married didn't stop the harassment I endured. Just a few weeks before our wedding, I flew first-class to Tokyo on a business trip. I had all-day meetings and field visits to research trials with seven Japanese men discussing weed control in rice. After the long day, they decided they wanted to take me out that night for a "bachelorette party," since I had mentioned to them that my wedding was coming up. Of course, there were no women with us—Japanese women didn't work in corporations, and wives never came to company dinners or outings. But I'd gotten along all right in Asia overall. With my title and identity as Dr. Jackson, I came off more as a neuter than as either a man or a woman, which was fine with me.

We headed out to a fancy Japanese restaurant, featuring low tables with cushions, dozens of trays of delicious food, and many glasses of room-temperature sake in traditional little *sakazuki* cups. The seven men, all married, were seated around the table but often hopped up to make toasts, sing me a song, and wish me congratulations on my approaching marriage. It was a bit raucous, but fun and sweet. I leaned back on the soft cushions, observing the festivities, thinking, *I'm getting married—I'm sexually off-limits, danger-free from harassment, in the married safety zone again*, as I tricked myself into forgetting the truth of the past.

As the upper manager of the group paid the exorbitant bill with his company credit card, several of the men proposed that we go to a nearby disco. They wanted to show me Japanese nightlife and music, and it seemed like a lark to me, since discos were really out of fashion in the United States by this time. We strolled down the street, and my hosts footed the over-the-top cover charge. As we entered the room of flashing strobe lights and mirror balls, I relived an atmosphere that screamed 1970.

We ordered drinks, stood around, and watched the dancers while they boogied down, until the manager of the group asked me to dance. It seemed harmless enough—it was all kind of a joke anyway. But then a slow dance came on and he gripped me close and murmured in my ear, "We should go somewhere alone together."

"No!" I said.

"Okay, then I'll just walk you home, back to your hotel," he offered.

Well, no, thank you. I had at least learned that was a cover for an attack, as the hotel incident from years earlier still rattled around in my brain.

Excusing myself, I trudged back to my hotel alone, dragging my feet, slumped down, and making passive-aggressive middle-finger signs under my coat.

Once again, the next morning came after a disturbing, sleepless night, and there was my harasser at the morning meeting, acting as if nothing had happened. I glared at him, and this time I didn't try to make it better for him with small talk. Thank God this was the last day of the business trip and I could head home to Craig and Dane that evening.

LEGAL AND SOCIAL GROWTH

IT TOOK COURT cases and lawsuits throughout the 1980s to enact the Pregnancy Discrimination Act of 1978. Westinghouse Electric Corporation settled a case with employees in 1980 that alleviated some of the company's discriminatory pregnancy policies and served as a model for other cases to come. The corporation ceased practices of termination, lost pay, loss of reinstatement, and denial of rehire rights when someone left because of pregnancy. And Westinghouse financially compensated employees who had been discriminated against with restored pay, seniority, and service time credits.

In addition to discrimination against the basic state of being pregnant, in the 1980s maternity leave was offered in only twelve states, and Missouri, where I lived at the time of my miscarriage, wasn't one of them. [3] After almost ten years of advocacy, the Family and Medical Leave Act (FMLA) was signed by then-president Bill Clinton in 1993. This law gave men and women job-protected leave for care of a newborn, newly adopted child, or ill family member, and for their own serious illness. However, the law did not require that employees receive any pay during their leave, and it pertained only to companies with more than fifty employees. That left many employees with no access to leave, which is still true today. The United States is the only high-income country in the world that does not mandate paid maternity leave, right there along with lower-income countries such as Suriname and New Guinea. [4]

Besides pregnancy and parental leave, the area of sexual harassment was a new focus of employment discrimination in the 1980s. In 1980, the EEOC wrote the first Guidelines on Discrimination Because of Sex and began to enforce that unwanted sexual advances were a type of sexual discrimination that was illegal under Title VII and created a hostile workplace. The guidelines defined two types of sexual harassment: (1) a quid pro quo, like I experienced back in the 1970s at Mr. Don's Restaurant, where a woman's job depends on her granting of sexual favors; and (2) a hostile work environment, such as I endured at multiple companies, where unwelcome sexual behavior or comments affect the workplace atmosphere. The most impactful part of the guidelines, issued in 1989, held employers liable for these workplace behaviors, including the conduct of their supervisors.

Court cases emerged every year after the issuance of the guidelines, starting in 1981 and continuing all through the '80s, as the courts dealt with the explosion of the number and variety of sexual harassment violations. [5] The case of *Bundy v. Jackson* in 1981 supported the EEOC's position that sexual insults and advances created a hostile work environment and constituted employment discrimination. Sandra Bundy, a vocational rehabilitation specialist at the District of Columbia Department of Corrections (DCDC), was sexually harassed by colleagues and supervisors, including Delbert Jackson, who later became the director of the DCDC. In her job, Bundy suffered repeated questions about her sexual desires, demands for sexual favors, and sexual advances from her supervisors. When she complained, she received poor performance reviews. She filed suit and lost because the court ruled that the harassment did not result in the loss of a job-related benefit. But on appeal, the court ruled that, under Title VII, sex discrimination included any harassment that affected the emotional and psychological work environment and created an intimidating, hostile, or offensive workplace. Bundy prevailed.

The Supreme Court reviewed its first sexual harassment case in 1986. Six years after the debut of the Guidelines on Discrimination Because of Sex, the court finally legitimized the guidelines when *Meritor Savings Bank v. Vinson* came before the judges. The court recognized sexual harassment as a valid claim, but none of us discussed it. We were busy working, were afraid to speak up, and didn't want to sabotage our careers. We knew we were lucky just to be in the boys' club.

Even though many of us were oblivious, the 1986 ruling was monumental in a number of ways. This was the first time that a sexual harassment case had been brought before the US Supreme Court. The case, *Meritor Savings Bank v. Vinson*, had to be really bad to get the attention of the court, and it was. Mechelle Vinson, a bank employee, was forced, on the threat of losing her job, to have sex with her boss up to fifty times in vaults and basements of the bank. The ruling in her favor was the precedent for all the similar cases that would follow. It made it clear that sexual harassment in the workplace is unacceptable. The court also stated that any employer that knew about unwanted sexual advances in the workplace was required to take action. Finally, it set the precedent for the "hostile environment" definition of sexual harassment—now, offensive remarks were grounds for a lawsuit.

The legal incidents in the 1980s regarding a "hostile work environment" resonated with me as I thought about all the episodes—Fried Eggs, grimaces about a miscarriage, rumors of fictitious affairs—that had ruined my day but that I couldn't really classify as rape or assault. I wasn't just crazy or overly sensitive or unable to take a joke. Now, the effect these behaviors had on a workplace and on a woman's ability to fully do her job was recognized. The crushing feeling in my chest that made it hard to breathe sometimes lifted a little.

Other external events both provoked and emboldened me in the 1980s. *Ms.* magazine celebrated its tenth anniversary. I marveled at Gloria Steinem's speeches about how women who stood up for their rights faced ridicule. She spoke about what little progress we had made in ten years, and I started thinking about what I could do to advance our cause, especially in the area of sexual harassment and discrimination.

The proposed Equal Rights Amendment (ERA) was not ratified by its June 1982 deadline, and I stalked around my house, punching pillows. All it said was, "Equality of rights under the law shall not be denied or abridged by the United States or any State on account of sex," but even that small statement was too much for thirty-eight states in America to accept. I gave each pillow an extra sock for Phyllis Schlafly, a woman against women, who campaigned heavily against the ERA with her claims that women wanted "to be treated like a woman, not like a man, and certainly not a sex-neutral 'person,'" and that the "ERA will do absolutely nothing for women in the field of employment." [6]

I started hearing women describe what offensive behavior in the workplace looked like, and I could certainly relate. I saw women speaking out and being heard, and that spurred me on to raise my voice and make personal changes of my own.

PART III

1990s–2010s

six

~~

THE CORPORATE LADDER

STANDING IN MY UNDERWEAR IN MY HOTEL ROOM ON
another business trip, ironing my male-uniform-equivalent
clothes for the next day—white blouse, beige wool suit—I
nearly burned my skirt, as my eyes were riveted to the *Hill v.
Thomas* hearing unfolding on screen. Law professor Anita Hill
alleged that Supreme Court justice nominee Clarence Thomas
sexually harassed her when she worked for him at, ironically,
the Equal Employment Opportunity Commission and the
Department of Education. Their 1991 hearing was all over the
news.

When my long workdays ended, I rushed to the hotel and
up the elevator, ordered room service, and watched night after
night as the all-male, all-white Senate Judiciary Committee
crucified Hill, labeling her as a spurned lover, an erotomaniac,
a racist, part of a political conspiracy, a glory-seeker, an over-
sensitive prude, vengeful, delusional, a mediocre worker, a ra-
bid feminist, a lesbian, and a whore who dressed provocatively.

Adding to the spectacle was the sexual paradigm that
hung over the trial, insinuating that the lust of Thomas, a
black man, was expected and the submission of Hill, a black
woman, was acceptable. I saw the committee and the press
make men the good guys, as if they were saying, *Men can't help
it—it's just natural. Men are attracted to women. Can't you take a*

compliment or a joke? Boy, are you ladies sensitive! I know each time I was harassed at work, I didn't feel complimented or amused. I felt like someone had just poured cold, dirty water over my head and held me hostage.

One panel member asked Hill, "Why didn't you report your harassment at the time? Why didn't you speak up before?" All I could think was, *Do you see what happens when we do?*

She had the courage to finally vocalize her harassment because she didn't think a man of Thomas's character deserved confirmation to the Supreme Court. Despite her selfless act, the final outcome was that Thomas was confirmed. He still sits on the Supreme Court in 2019, despite his history of sexual harassment. Later, I learned that back at her job at the University of Oklahoma College of Law after the hearing, Hill was subjected to demands that she resign and attempts to revoke her tenure.

The hearing brought out my worst fears and, even in my anger, made me more afraid than ever to reveal my harassment experiences. The whole ugly scene left me thinking, *Yeah, I know that men want to keep their power and they want me and other women to go away. I know it doesn't matter how men behave—the man is right, and the woman is always wrong. The woman suffers more if she complains. And it is so clear to me now what happens when we tell on men. I can't talk about any of my past sexual harassment incidents. I'm terrified of possible defamation of character, loss of all my hard work, and all the potential repercussions if I say anything. Women who tell on men can lose their jobs, their reputations, and their careers. But, Anita, despite Thomas's denials and the white-man committee's blundering, I believe you.*

I was in the minority. Polls at the time showed that more than 60 percent of Americans believed Thomas, not Hill. [1]

My sister and I talked daily on the phone about the outrage of this travesty. Our mother was on Clarence Thomas's side in some strange way, making comments like "Poor Clarence—he was probably just flirting a little or trying to be complimentary. Poor men—they don't know how they're supposed to behave these days. I feel so sorry for them. Women are always on them about something." Was she experiencing a kind of Patty Hearst-esque Stockholm syndrome, in which a captive identifies and sympathizes with her captors? Our mother had been suppressed by men all her life, a real slave to her husband's master role, yet she defended the status quo. "I like the way things are with men in their roles and women in theirs. I like having men open doors for me," she would say.

DESPITE THE MOCKERY going on in the news, I leaped out of bed each morning, practiced yoga, and kissed Craig. We dropped off Dane at school and then commuted together, chatting the whole way, to our Fortune 500 jobs. At my new company, freshly married, I loved arriving each day to greet my staff, button up my white lab coat, and play in the greenhouses and laboratories where we worked with chemists designing new and more environmentally sound pesticides. When my Agricultural Chemicals group was sold to one of my past Fortune 500 employers, the company moved me to the energy side of its business, into a nonscience position. When the corporation downsized, they asked, "So, what else can you do?" When I said I'd taught, they fashioned me into a trainer for delivering health, environment, and safety information to employees.

I started getting harangued for having a PhD, an honor that was supposed to belong to men. Of course, now I see it was another form of retaliation for my having violated the female norm. It was not usual for a woman to have a graduate degree, especially among high school- or bachelor-degreed men.

"You don't need a PhD like Lucinda to understand this project. In fact, it's probably better if we're not too academic about this," I would hear.

Or, "You ivory-tower types don't have a grasp of the real world," they would say.

Sexual discrimination remained the norm. One of my bosses took the whole team (all men) out for a fishing trip for the weekend but didn't invite me. The following Monday, there they were, recapping: "Wow, what a catch George made! Great time on Saturday. Boy, was I drunk! But I'm so glad we worked out who's going to lead the new Utah project."

I burned inside. *I wanted to manage the Utah project. How dare they make important work decisions in my absence? I can't believe I didn't even get a chance to plead my case.*

A week later, my supervisor beckoned me to his office and asked me if I felt left out about the fishing trip. "My wife pointed out to me that you might feel that way," he said.

"Yeah, of course I felt left out," I said, but didn't elaborate, trying to play it cool.

"But you always said you were on the side of the fish. I figured you didn't like to fish," he said.

"Well, no, I don't," I said, "but that's not the point; it's that . . . Oh, never mind." I could see his eyes widening and mouth gaping with fear that we were about to have a long, painful, and potentially career-limiting conversation. I didn't have the energy for it and just traipsed out of his office, thinking, *It's not worth it to try to educate him. I'm a short-timer. This training job isn't a good fit. I miss science. I need to find a new job and a new boss.*

After that conversation, I began calling everyone I knew

for insights into other jobs in the company. I applied, interviewed, re-interviewed, and hounded the job owners for any position related even remotely to science. With my motto of "Do at least one thing every day, no matter how small—even a phone call—toward getting a new job," I finagled my way back into a science position, capitalizing on my biology and environmental background. But I remained a threat. I had the credentials of most of my colleagues again, but I had also become outspoken and unafraid to advocate for projects and points of view that I believed were right, such as making the business case for environmental projects when many saw them as a cost, rather than a cost savings. My supervisor wrote on my annual review, "Lucinda always follows through and backs up her words with action, like on the Thailand project. She pushed for a new approach, aligned with customers, and speedily implemented the Colombia and Bangladesh projects, saving five million dollars for the company, then successfully completed all milestones and key metrics." I gave my opinion, questioned things, and advocated for change. All of these traits made my male colleagues see me as a true competitor who might take their job.

SOLIDLY BACK IN science, a male-dominated field, in a male-dominated company, I saw that as women rise up the corporate ladder, so does sexual discrimination. I had to negotiate and demand every promotion I ever got; never was a position advancement or raise just "given" to me. I always had top ratings, but I received comments such as "Well, Lucinda, you don't need the money, and David here has a wife and children to support."

At lower levels, we aren't a big threat; men will put up

with us and still think it's nice to have a woman or two around. But as I moved up, it became cutthroat, and there was a real fear that I might actually get a certain job, instead of a man. And there are few women at the top, so when I did land a high-level leadership role in global environmental management, I was again the sole female at the table. Even into the 2010s, I was the lone woman on my leadership team, the lone woman in the ladies' room as the men bonded over their peeing.

I obsessed about the number of women in the room. In every meeting, I would count the women and figure out the ratio and the percentage on my napkin: 1:22 (5 percent); 2:50 (4 percent); 3:40 (8 percent, a good day). I still was often the only one of my kind in the room, and old, chilling visions of me in my fancy purple dress, entering a room full of men, shot through my mind and caused heart tremors. One time, I was in a meeting with all women, maybe six to seven of us, and a feeling of complete calm came over me. We weren't interrupting each other, fighting for floor space. No one said, "Oh, I'm so glad that Ted brought that up," crediting a woman's idea to a man. We all breathed easily, and I could have hugged every one of them. It was a rare event that's permanently stored among my best memories.

Women in the corporate workplace had—and still have—a tendency to try to fit in as one of the boys, in hopes that it might earn us some of the advantages that men have. I remember one meeting where, as I sat in a dreary conference room, three women managers charged in to give us a presentation. They all looked like men—all short haircuts and gray, manly suits. What a shame—we were all afraid to express an ounce of conventional femininity, as that could lead to sexual harassment or a perceived diminishment of our power. I saw women swearing and laughing at sex jokes and working hard to memorize football scores so they could participate in coffee-room conversations.

Around that time, I decided to be more myself. I starting wearing dresses, jewelry, a stylish jacket, and high heels to work, instead of a square-fitting pantsuit and the female version of wingtips that we women had adopted. The look was still corporate, but with a little flair. My male coworkers noticed, telling me, "You look energetic and good today."

And they were right. I thought, *Yeah, a little personal authenticity goes a long way toward making you feel better about yourself.* It was a tiny forward step in the growth of my self-confidence and toward reclaiming my feminine identity, which I had stuffed down for a long time in my attempt to fit in with the majority. I noticed that as I took that chance, younger women in the office saw me as a role model and began dressing more individually themselves.

AT ONE POINT, while working on an internal diversity study for my corporation, I took a statistical and science-based look at the numbers to eke out the truth about women in the corporate workplace. There was a long-held assumption that women left corporate jobs to have babies and thus were not abundant in the upper ranks. The data showed that men and women were hired equally, and in the first few years of their careers were represented about fifty-fifty in the workforce population. But about five to ten years later, at a certain higher career level, the number of women dropped drastically—and that trend continued until only a handful existed at the highest levels of a company. The same occurred for minority men, though at a slightly later time in their careers. The data also showed that women left not to have babies but for other, higher-level jobs elsewhere, or to start their own businesses. They left because they were sidelined, not promoted, shuffled off to noncore projects.

With these results in hand, the executive team concluded that women just needed to wait longer—that promotion is in the pipeline; it will all work out. We modeled it and found that, at our current rate of progress, it would take twenty-five years to move women up even one pay level. The executive committee we presented our results to did not embrace the actions we proposed, such as documented exit interviews, key technical assignments for women, and championing women to fill international jobs. But in specific departments with forward-looking managers, these things were starting to take place.

One of my primary observations during this period was that discrimination can be harder to spot at the top. There, men are more careful and less obvious about their discrimination and harassment. In one job, my boss, Barry, was decent, with daughters and a strong wife. I was lulled into thinking he was nonsexist. He never harassed me, but he had the sexist gene in him, though I didn't see it right away. One of the vice presidents, Mike, was disrespectful and condescending to me, and I confided in Barry. He was sympathetic, coaching me on how to deal with it and telling me to stay strong, preserve my beliefs, continue to stand up for myself.

I was the only woman on his leadership team of fifteen managers, but I excused him for that continuing imbalance, thinking, *Okay, I know certain technical fields don't attract many women, so, as positions arise, maybe he tries to recruit women but none apply or he can't find any.* But when his human resources position was vacant, he selected a man; then his legal position opened up and he selected a man. I mulled it over. *Women dominate both of those fields. He had to go out of his way to find a man. His leadership team intentionally will remain 100 percent male, except for me. And I'm here only because he "inherited" me from his predecessor.*

As I saw this happening, I realized how much more comfortable most men are with other men, and I grew wary. But I still assumed Barry was on my side. I fought for thorough examination of our division's diversity statistics and demographics, trying to ensure equal treatment of women and minority men, and Barry nodded his head in support. But in the end, I faced retaliation. It was quite personal and hurtful to me, who still relied so much on approval. We got rated each year, and I still went after the "A," just like I had in school. I had always received high marks my whole career. But this time my rating was reduced to a lower tier. Barry said it was because I had stood up to my superior Mike and hadn't agreed with the corporate line that Mike wanted. *You hypocrite! You betrayer!* I thought. *You were the one who encouraged me to fight in the first place!* I believed he was a feminist of some sort, but it turned out in the end that he was for the man all along. A woman can be told in one breath to speak up for herself and in the next can be reprimanded for being too demanding and strong.

Another time, one of my companies offered its employees a severance package because it was downsizing. I found out that several men on the same level as I were leaving and receiving a sizable financial package, so it struck me as a good opportunity to exit the organization. But when I applied for the severance, I was told it wasn't available to me. When I started to question that, management took a defensive stance and changed their story several times. When I couldn't get a clear reason about why I wasn't eligible, I went to Human Resources, then elevated it to Executive Human Resources and fought it.

The company began saying I wasn't authorized for the

package because of my age, since I was older than the men who were leaving and would likely be retiring at some unspecified point in the future. So now I was also a victim of age discrimination, as well as gender bias. Of course, all those biases are interwoven. Younger women may think their careers are going great, but they don't realize the old boys' club is alive and well; men stick together and really don't want us in the workplace, jousting against them. We're fine at the lower, nonthreatening levels, but if we try to compete equally and maybe "take" a job from one of them, they hate it. There are fewer and fewer jobs at the top, so if they can get rid of one group of competitors—like women—easily, then all the better.

But I challenged this discrimination and won. I had truly grown and developed from unworthy to strong by then. I went from my manager to Human Resources to the vice president of Human Resources to the ombudsman (who was an ombudswoman) to two lawyers, and got my shit together, fought for myself, and carried off my prize.

Finally, unlike my 1970s experience with the male lawyer who told me not to pursue a lawsuit, there were now plenty of amazing, experienced women attorneys who specialized in employment law and gender discrimination. They were instantly supportive and educated me on my rights and options.

And many companies have an ombudsperson now—a neutral, high-ranking figure who is not part of executive management, to whom employees can go for help resolving ethical concerns in their workplace. The ombudsperson provides objective coaching, options, solutions, and recommendations for procedure changes. My ombudsperson helped me maneuver the channels and come out with an equitable solution. I highly recommend that women use the legal and ombudsperson resources available to them today. Unfortunately,

Human Resources is not always your friend. The job of HR people is to protect the company, and nothing you say to them is confidential.

I celebrated with a glass of wine with Craig that I had pursued this and beaten the system. And, not satisfied with a win just for me, I learned from one of the lawyers that I could negotiate policy as part of the settlement. I asked the company to clarify its severance and age discrimination policies per the Age Discrimination in Employment Act. I could leave a legacy. I cracked this age- and gender-bias thing open for those coming after me, so that others wouldn't be discriminated against because of their age and sex.

I TRUDGED RUNG by rung up the corporate ladder and catapulted into the corner office. The ladder part was a slog, as I strategically gained required experience in vision setting, management, people skills, and budgets. The catapult part was a calculated, concerted effort to jump onto the executive platform. I spotted the job I wanted—head of all health, environment, and safety research and technical expertise in the company—and kept close track of it for several years. I ensured that I understood the qualifications for the job and filled in any gaps in my résumé. I knew who the incumbent was and when he might leave or retire. I examined possible competitors, evaluated their skills, and considered how I might win out over them. I engaged anyone who might be on the selection committee. I wrote the job on my long-term-goals document and told every upper-management person I knew that I was interested in that position. When the job finally became available, I was right there.

Over the years, I protected and helped other women. It was something I could do as my professional status rose, and in some ways, it was easier than helping myself. Even in a room full of men, I could call them on obvious sexism. Once, I had a woman employee who wanted an assignment in Indonesia. She was totally qualified for the job, but I was told she couldn't do it because she was single and there were no single women in the location—though, of course, there were single men. I kept questioning the logic, pushing, accusing, and finally got the job for her. She was successful there for many years.

I saw a woman up for promotion who was not considered because it was announced to a room full of men that she was out on disability—on maternity leave. All the men nodded. "Yes, of course, that's a plausible reason to knock her off the list."

I pointed out that it was illegal to discuss why someone was out on disability—would they have said, "Steve is out with a broken leg, so let's not promote him?"—and that it was also illegal to discriminate against that person because of it. After much back-and-forth, Human Resources and Legal finally spoke up and said I was right. The men reluctantly put her back on the list, and her promotion was approved.

One of the most important tips I shared with women over the years is that they don't have to tell all. A young female employee would come into my office and say, "I'm planning on having a baby next year. I'm going to tell my supervisor about my plans so he can plan for my absence on disability leave. Also, my husband might be getting another job in two years, so I'm going to let my supervisor know we might be moving."

Or, "I know international assignments are important, but I can't really move anywhere because of my husband's job, so I'm writing here on my performance review that I'm not mobile."

Or, "I've got a swim meet for my daughter on Tuesday, and I have to work in the snack shack, so I'm going to tell my boss that I can't come to our afternoon staff meeting."

"Wait," I'd say. "Too much information. First, you don't know for sure if and when you'll get pregnant, so don't bring it up right now. Second, your husband might not get the job, so who knows if you'll be moving or not? Third, your husband's job might change in the future, or he might decide he wants an international adventure, so there's no need to say now that you aren't available for a global assignment. You're not telling a lie or keeping a secret—it's just that you don't know what will actually happen in the future—so don't mention it. It will just make your bosses discount you for future assignments."

As for the swim meet, I'd counsel, "Your snack shack duties that interfere with your staff meeting will reinforce existing prejudices that females should be mothers, not career women, and that we can't give as much to our jobs as men can. If it's that important to you to go, tell your boss you have an appointment; you don't need to give details unless he asks. As for the snack shack, I've had that job, and it's awful. If I were you, I'd recruit somebody else to do it!"

I never advise women to lie. Women have lived their lives as lies for so many years. We lie about our capabilities, our true feelings; we pretend and manipulate in order to gain male favor or bolster men's egos. I relished when I started really telling the truth about myself. I started realizing I could win that tennis game, ace that test, meet the top metric for that project, and show who I truly was. I didn't have to giggle when I wasn't amused or smile when I was mad or meet gender expectations programmed into me. I advise telling the truth, but you don't have to offer up everything in your mind and heart, not all the gritty details.

As the only woman on a selection team, I fought for the woman who was recommended to be taken off the candidate list because the men, as they said, "didn't like her voice—it was too high and annoying." With persuasion and objection to discrimination on my part, she got the job and was a top performer in the company.

Another woman was not given the funding she was entitled to for going back to school. Her supervisor flat-out denied it, for no legal reason, so I reprimanded him, went to Human Resources, and got her the financial reimbursement she deserved to earn an advanced degree.

When we finished promotions for the year, I made sure we went back and looked at our diversity statistics. Had we promoted all white men? If so, why? Had we missed any women or minorities? Inevitably, gender or racial bias had crept in and needed to be adjusted. It's called "unconscious bias," but I still suspect a lot of it is conscious.

And when I left a job, I tried to ensure a "power transfer" of woman to woman. In all my positions in corporate America, I was the first woman ever to have the job I had; I always succeeded a man. Once I had shown that, by God, a woman could do the job, I had a chance to jump on it and be sure it didn't revert to being a "man's job." That didn't mean a man could never have the job again in the future, of course, but it was satisfying when my successor was a woman. Otherwise, it was easily seen as a fluke that one woman had made it. I worked hard at mentoring, planting the seeds, participating on the selection committees, and was successful many times in making sure a qualified woman came after me. There were always a number of female candidates, often those who had been overlooked but who had amazing credentials, when someone like me took the time to advocate for them.

The men in charge came up with so many excuses for what a woman lacked, so many catch-22s. For example, if employees didn't have any international experience, they couldn't get promoted or moved up to higher-level jobs—but then, international assignments weren't available to women. I saw top-notch women engineers recommended for training jobs because "women make good teachers"—but training jobs had no room for growth. Then they couldn't get the next engineering job because they had been in a training job, not a "real" engineer job, and so on and so on. But I fought for every one of those women and for the most part was effective. It just takes someone having the guts to call the boys on their bad behavior. My experience is that, if they can, men will discriminate, and if no one takes them to task for it, so much the better. But if someone does speak out, they'll back down and capitulate and justice can be served.

Speaking out and questioning the status quo is a way for everyone to learn and agree on right and wrong behaviors. As women rise up the corporate ladder and gain more power, we can argue that employees who misbehave, such as by showing blatant sexism or prejudices, shouldn't get that promotion or should even be fired. We can seek justice, rather than revenge. We can push back as equals. And as we attain equality, we have an obligation as women to help other women and minorities. It doesn't mean we have to advocate for everyone at all costs; it means we should open a door for those who deserve it.

SURVIVAL OF LEGAL AND SOCIAL CHANGE

SEXUAL HARASSMENT-RELATED challenges and liabilities for corporations and government mounted during the 1990s and 2000s. Kerry Ellison, an Internal Revenue Service employee, filed a lawsuit against Nicolas Brady, secretary of the US Department of the Treasury, alleging that a male coworker had sent her love letters that he believed were not offensive. However, Ellison found them objectionable—and it was ruled that this exchange could legitimately create a hostile working environment. In 1991, in *Ellison v. Brady*, the court decided that the standard in sexual harassment cases must be defined by the perspective of a "reasonable woman," not a "reasonable person." This case redefined sexual harassment by considering the victim's point of view, rather than convention. The concept was reinforced in 1991 in *Robinson v. Jacksonville Shipyards*, in which the woman found the use of crude language and pornography offensive. These acts were ruled a violation of Title VII.

Just months after the *Hill v. Thomas* hearing, the Civil Rights Act of 1991 passed and Congress modified Title VII. Now, sexual harassment victims had the right to a jury trial in federal court and the right to seek damage awards, such as back pay, reinstatement, and compensatory and punitive damages. This development spurred action within the EEOC and the courts. In the yearly quarter following the *Hill v. Thomas* hearing and the Civil Rights Act of 1991, filings of sexual harassment with the EEOC increased by a dramatic 71 percent, compared with the same quarter a year prior. [2] The number of sexual harassment cases in the United States rose from 6,883 in 1991 to 15,618 in 1998, more than doubling. [3] In 1995, one of the largest settlements in a harassment case against a corporation at the time occurred when Chevron Corporation's Information Technology Company settled for $2.2 million with four women who experienced sexual advances and pornography in the workplace. The year after that, Chevron settled for $7.4 million with 777 women for sexual harassment and discrimination. Companies began to face more requirements—as part of the 1996 harassment case, Chevron

Corporation also had to establish diversity councils, hire high-level ombudspersons, and institute career guidance programs. Awards to victims have gone from a few million dollars in the '90s, under federal law, to a high of $168 million in 2012, to Ani Chopourian in *Chopourian v. Catholic Healthcare West*, likely the largest judgment in American history awarded to a single victim. [4]

Key Supreme Court decisions on sexual harassment in 1998 put more onus on employers. If the harasser were in a superior position in the company, compared with the victim, and a negative job action occurred against the employee, the company was liable. And same-sex harassment was now illegal in the workplace.

That same year, the Supreme Court ruled on guidance for mandatory sexual harassment training for businesses and governments. However, it was up to individual states to enforce the ruling, and it took seven years for the first state, California, to do so, requiring it for all employers with more than fifty employees. As of 2018, sexual harassment training is still not required for companies in forty-six states. Only California, Connecticut, Maine, and New York mandate it. And New York State didn't even join this list until 2018, twenty years after the Supreme Court ruling.

OTHER HIGH-PROFILE cases like the 1991 *Hill v. Thomas* trial flashed on the nightly news and increased the general public's awareness of how things were changing. I sat watching all this on the couch while nursing my new baby, Troy, and then my next baby, Weston, during the '90s, exhausted but tingling with excitement that sexual harassment was coming out into the open after so many years of silence. There was the Navy Tailhook scandal in 1992, when male Navy and Marine personnel harassed eighty-three women, including Navy officers, at a convention at a Hilton Hotel in Las Vegas. The Hilton lost a $5.2 million lawsuit for failing to provide security, and several of the offending officers lost their jobs. Oregon senator Bob Packwood resigned in 1995 after twenty-nine women pressed charges against him for sexual assault and harassment. Paula Jones brought a sexual harassment lawsuit against Bill Clinton, whom she accused of having her escorted to his hotel room in Arkansas, where he exposed himself to her and propositioned her. The case was settled out of court in 1998 for $850,000, but it demonstrated that even the president of the United States could be charged with sexual harassment; I cheered that no one was exempt from the law.

These sensational cases continued on in the 2000s. In 2007, Anucha Browne Sanders, an executive for the New York Knicks, sued Madison Square Garden et al. for sexual harassment and retaliation after she was fired for reporting it. The charge was against Isiah Thomas, the head coach and president of basketball operations for the Knicks, for making sexually demeaning comments and soliciting her for sex. The federal court jury awarded Browne Sanders $11.6 million in punitive damages; they settled out of court for $11.5 million that ended all appeals.

The blame for sexual harassment remained primarily on the victim, however, and most of us were afraid of speaking out. There was still the rule that the victim had to prove that the harassment was so atrocious that it caused severe psychological damage. Another catch-22—if we women proved that the harassment destroyed us mentally and emotionally, we would never be employable again, given the prejudices surrounding mental illness. In 1993, the Supreme Course case of

Harris v. Forklift Systems, Inc. finally put a stop to this kind of judgment against the victim—she didn't need to have a mental disorder to make her point. Blame was back where it belonged—on the harasser and the workplace environment that a company fostered by allowing the harassment. However, the court clarified that an offensive joke or comment was not grounds for a sexual harassment lawsuit—it had to be something more traumatic.

Then, in 1994, the courts ruled that "she's a whore anyway" claims about the sexual history of victims could be limited in testimony. I was frightened in the 1970s when the lawyer told me I would ruin my reputation and get pulled through the mud if I sued my employer. Twenty years later, something was done about it. Now, the Violence Against Women Act of 1994 ensured that the sexual history of a person bringing forth a harassment charge was limited as evidence. The act did, however, permit the use of sexual history of the harasser accused of assault.

Another win for victims occurred in the 2009 case *Crawford v. Metropolitan Government of Nashville and Davidson County*. The Human Resources department of the organization launched an investigation of Gene Hughes, the Employee Relations director for the Metro School District, for sexual harassment. Vicky Crawford, one of his employees, was called in and relayed incidents of harassment she had encountered with Hughes. She was subsequently fired. The ruling in this case protects from retaliation employees, such as Crawford, who merely cooperated with an internal probe, rather than reported an offense on their own. This case was critical in encouraging bystanders and witnesses of sexual harassment to speak up.

Of course, setbacks for the victim and breaks for companies balanced the wins. Barbara Landgraf was harassed from

1984 to 1986 by her colleague at USI Film Products in Texas. She was found to be a victim of sexual harassment and a hostile workplace when she filed a case in 1989 but wasn't granted any compensation because the law at that time didn't authorize recovery of damages. After the passage of the Civil Rights Act of 1991, which granted the right to a jury trial and both punitive and compensatory damages to victims of sexual harassment, Landgraf appealed her case. But the Supreme Court ruled in 1994's *Landgraf v. USI Film Products* that the Civil Rights Act of 1991 applied only to future cases and wasn't retroactive. So, essentially, if our harassment occurred before 1991, like much of mine did, we couldn't receive any compensation.

In 1997, in *Farley v. American Cast Iron Pipe Company*, the US court of appeals ruled that if a company had a strict sexual harassment policy, it wouldn't be held liable for harassment in its workplace unless the harassment was reported and the company did not take action.

In 2000, there was a ruling that a victim had to demonstrate that the sexual advances she received in her workplace were not welcome. In *Baldwin v. Blue Cross Shield of Alabama*, Susan Baldwin sued for a hostile work environment and retaliation when she was fired for reporting harassment. Even though she had ample evidence of unwanted, lewd name calling and antics, the incidents were deemed "not sufficiently outrageous as a matter of Alabama law." [5] Baldwin's case was dismissed in 2007, and the dismissal was upheld later in appellate courts, creating a legal precedent for other judges to reject similar cases. The *Ellison v. Brady* case of 1991, in which the court decided that the standard in sexual harassment cases must be defined by the perspective of a "reasonable woman," not a "reasonable person," lost ground.

Both to capture the mood of the era and to relieve some of my own stress during this time, I dashed off corporate poems in between meetings (or during the tedious ones):

Invisible
Did I just speak?
Was I the only one who heard?
Until what I just said was repeated by a male
And everyone
Praised
Him

Only Two of Us
Only two of us in the workplace
Yet they can't keep us straight
"Betsy, come here"
"Tell Theo I said hi"
Yet my name is Kay and
I am married to John

New Job, or Everything Was Going Well
Everything was going
So well
A new opportunity
I think I got the job!
Until,
Rising to leave
He gives me
An inappropriate hug
And says, "I'm a hugger"

seven

~⌒

BOY CHILDREN

MY RELATIONSHIP WITH CRAIG WORKED OUT. AS OF THE
writing of this book, we've been married almost thirty years,
and we raised three wonderful boys. I had a goal to nurture
them into liberated men, and my husband and I scored 100
percent with all three of them. Sweet success. Our techniques
were simple. We loved them unconditionally and talked about
everything. We taught them to be proud of themselves and of
us. And we kept on top of the small behaviors that could turn
into bigger, sexist attitudes later on.

One of my boys was at a friend's family's house when he
was in college. After dinner, my son tried to help clear the table. The father said, "Don't do that. That's what you boys get a
wife for," in front of my son, his college-age son, his two
teenage boys, and his wife.

Later that evening, when they were hanging out, my son
mentioned to his friend, "Uh, that was a little sexist."

His friend replied, "What?"

"You know, what your dad said about getting a wife to do
menial work for you."

"Oh, really? I didn't know that."

My point is that there are mothers and fathers today raising sexist boys, so there will still be plenty of sexist men in the
future. But we can change that. We need to make a pledge to

raise liberated boys. I know it's hard; I know many women are afraid to stand up to men, especially their husbands and partners. Just as my mother was, women are often financially dependent on men and frightened that they might lose what little security they've managed to scavenge for themselves.

But we can't let it continue. Though it's sad that women remain the main child-rearing force in families today, we can leverage that position to raise nonsexist children. Women have so much influence over their kids. I encourage all women to take advantage of that to change the next generation of men. No matter how rough-and-tumble your husband or your boys may be, you can have a heavy impact on how they turn out—a real "Mama, Don't Let Your Cowboys Grow Up to Be Sexist" effect.

MY SINGLE MOTHER status afforded learning opportunities for many years to my oldest son, Dane. He saw that his mother could do anything; he observed a woman buying and selling a house, purchasing a car, running a household, taking care of the yard, and working full-time. He saw me dating—and crying over—men and started to recognize the ones who weren't trustworthy or committed. One man, Jake, developed a close relationship with both me and Dane, when Dane was four years old, but then decided a long-term commitment wasn't for him. To explain Jake's absence, I told Dane, "We won't be seeing Jake for a while; he needs his privacy and doesn't want to be with me right now. But you and I are a family already, and we will always be a family and have each other. Jake still loves us, especially you."

Dane said, "Well, I hate him. I'm going to turn him into a rat! I don't care if he loves us—my heart is already broken.

When your heart is broken, it means you don't love somebody anymore."

Dane's bluntness and matter-of-factness actually buoyed my self-esteem and helped me recover more quickly from the rejection. *Yeah*, I thought. *Dane, you're right!*

"Mom, you can draw ThunderCats as good as Jake," he added.

If you have a partner in parenting, who you select is monumental in raising liberated boys, so pay close attention to that choice. I consciously picked Craig because he was considerate and not macho, but still strong. Since I had a seven-year-old child when I started dating him, I got to see his parenting style ahead of marriage. The first time he came over to our house, he brought live reptiles for Dane to touch—a child's dream. Dane loved the strange, big lizards whose heads looked just like their tails, so you couldn't tell if they were coming or going—the palindrome of the reptile world. Dane's eyes lit up, and his wide smile at this new man told me that Craig was thinking and caring about my son.

Craig showed up at a good time in my life, as I juggled work and daycare, struggling to raise Dane alone. Since it was just the two of us, Dane was my whole world—and he was becoming a small tyrant because of my doting. Craig tolerated McDonald's, but Dane didn't get to choose that venue every time the three of us went out. When Craig observed that our tuck-in routine extended all evening, with bath, playtime, dessert, multiple long adventure stories, backrubs, teeth brushing, snacks, and repeated teeth brushing, he helped me streamline it from an average of two hours a night to half that time, while increasing child self-responsibility and instituting a more soothing, bonding, quality experience for everyone.

As our family grew to two more sons, all three boys saw

that their father could fix cars, build forts, and maneuver a full wheelbarrow—but they also saw him cry. He told them he loved them every day. He said, "I'm proud of you," and cherished who they were fundamentally. Even though Craig liked working on machines and conducting scientific experiments, he didn't insist they do everything he did, didn't ridicule them or say it wasn't manly if they wanted to draw or read instead. Boy Scouts played a big role in their development, too. I fought joining Scouts at first, thinking it was geeky and militaristic—my impressions from the 1960s. But it turned out to be a path to build confidence and leadership skills, for boys to know just a little more than the average urban kid, and to learn useful techniques, such as how to build a fire. Our sons took care of younger boys, and we picked a boy-led troop so they could learn what it was like to be in charge. They had chances to hike, camp, and scuba-dive, and Craig participated in all of it to cement father–son bonds.

In our house, it was, "Dad, what's for dinner?" And when they asked, "Where's Mom?" Craig replied, "She's out mowing the lawn." I still have the ticket stubs from one moonlit night when my boys and I went to see the San Francisco Giants play and watched Barry Bonds hit a homer into McCovey Cove. Their dad doesn't relish baseball, so I was on deck. But Craig prepared the cheese-and-cracker and Gatorade snack for soccer practice the next morning. In our mixed roles, neither of us dominated the other. We made decisions together. Craig and I were equal partners in wage earning, housework, driving kids, playing with them, disciplining—we always tried to present a united front.

I championed my career as a real positive to my boys and let them know how much I loved my work so they could see how a career is meaningful to both women and men. A typical before-trip conversation at the dinner table went like this: "You know I'm leaving for Argentina in the morning. It's in South America. See where it is on the map? Where is that in relation to our house? I'm going there to understand how we can restore an area's native plants. I'm meeting with a number of botanists from the university who know the local vegetation and can help me accomplish that. Let's look up what kids your age like to do there. I bet they have games and toys that we don't have here."

I called regularly from wherever I traveled, and we'd marvel at the feat of talking across the oceans. They liked the local toys and photos of kids in other states and countries that I brought back from my trips, and we'd talk about commonalities and differences. When I came to their classes to discuss and explain my career, they bragged to their friends about me. I purposely celebrated my professional successes, like a promotion or even a compliment, at home and included the boys, so they would know that their mother got trophies and awards, too. I gave subtle messages that I worked with all men and that I was challenging the status quo just by being there. When they were teenagers, I rapped to them as I left for work, "I'm heading off to work, mon, trying to get my freak on. The boys upstairs try to tell me what to wear." They hated it, but they still remember those lines today.

We encouraged all kinds of diverse experiences. I'd once seen my brother roughed up in his band uniform for being a sissy who played the trombone, so I wanted our boys to play in the school band, experience music, and discount any macho gender roles. Craig had played the violin as a child, so he role-modeled that not all boys play the guitar or drums. The boys went out for sports, but it wasn't a requirement and we didn't make a big deal about winning or dominating. If they got medals or ribbons, we congratulated them, but we didn't worship the kids who got more. Swim team was mixed gender, so they got to see strong girls competing.

We kept all girl-related messages positive. We never teased them if they liked a girl, and we treated all girls as friends. We never used the terms "sissy" or "like a girl." We consciously avoided saying things like, "She is so pretty" and focused on questions such as "Is she smart?" or "What does she like to do?" We also didn't make girls special by saying things like, "Never hit a girl" or, "Always be polite to girls." We expected our sons to treat everyone well. Our motto was "No bullying of any kind of anyone." We never laughed at mean teasing or tickling—it's not funny. And we were against all hitting, biting, angry words, and name calling of boys or girls.

We had pets, and our boys learned to appreciate them, since we had always viewed caring for animals as a sign of sensitivity. We had witnessed kids in our own childhood who tortured cats or reveled in impaling frogs, and we wanted to teach our sons that just because you're bigger and stronger, you don't have the right to harm someone small and vulnerable.

We didn't obsess about their toys. We included "boy toys," gender-neutral toys, and "girl toys" in their collection. We encouraged stuffed animals and dolls that they could sleep with for comfort, but also Legos, cars, and all kinds of games. We picked books that showed feelings and kindness, talked about how nicely a character in a book behaved, and explained why that was noble. They put their boy twist on the toys, with Beanie Baby battles and castles blowing up, but at least it was every Beanie Baby for himself or herself. I don't remember any boy–girl battles, and the girl Beanie Babies were just as wild as the boys. Even better, most of the time the Beanies had no gender at all; it just didn't matter.

Craig and I taught them that kindness and love to others was a feat of strength: Are you strong enough to help someone who needs help? Strong enough to befriend a lonely kid who needs a friend? If a classmate whom they didn't know or particularly like invited them over, we made them go anyway—at least once—to find out something good about that person. There were plenty of cliques at their schools that didn't associate with outcasts, loners, shy, or just "uncool" kids, and we fought against that by making our sons aware of those students and showing them how to exhibit friendship and empathy toward them. It didn't always work, but at least it made them sensitive to others.

Other parents often asked me, especially in junior high and high school, "Wow! How did you do that? I just saw your son give you a hug and kiss and tell you he loved you when you dropped him off. I could never get my boys to do that."

My answer was, "Never let them stop." I told the boys early on that it was part of their job description as my kids, and I didn't let a day go by when they didn't have to do it. It was all in fun—"Tell your adoring mother that you love her!"—but they still do it today, as men, so it worked.

We talked about everything. If someone's feelings got hurt, we sat down and discussed how they were feeling and how others felt. If they hurt my feelings, I told them that wasn't okay and demanded that we all speak respectfully to each other. We let them show a wide range of feelings—sad, mad, protective, comforting. "It's all right to cry," we told them.

We also insisted that they care about each other. The two older boys brought their baby brothers for Sharing Time in their classrooms and demonstrated how to care for them, such as by identifying how often a baby eats, cries, and poops and what you should do about it. We had a phrase, "brothers forever," that we used after a fight when they had to make up. It communicated to them how important siblings are for their whole lives.

I let them know that they could ask me anything, and I proved it by not flinching when they asked about penises or vaginas. I wanted them to know sex was a two-way street and should be enjoyable for both partners. One son told me years later that he clearly remembered asking me about the location and purpose of the clitoris, and I gave him valuable information: "If you can find it, it will make your future girlfriend very happy."

Every morning, we drove by protestors waving signs at an abortion clinic we passed on the way to elementary school. The first time, my sons peered out the car windows and asked, "What are those men doing?"

I explained, "They're protesting the right for women to decide if they want to have a baby or not. Those men think they, not the woman, should decide that she must have a baby if she gets pregnant."

"Why should they get to decide?" they asked.

"Well, I don't think they should. It's not fair to women. I think both women and men should get to make decisions about their own bodies."

The clinic also gave me an opportunity for another discussion. I got their attention with "You know, boys get pregnant, too."

"What? That isn't right, Mom—boys can't get pregnant!"

"Yes, they can. Because if you get a woman pregnant, it's your baby too, so you're both pregnant. You have to be even more responsible for conceiving a baby, because if you get someone pregnant, the woman decides whether you're a father or not. She might decide to have the baby, even if you don't want the child, so she calls the shots on this one. You need to be educated about birth control. Never have sex without birth control if you don't want to become a father."

Mainstream gender roles and attitudes seeped in, despite our positive practices at home. The boys created this god-awful game they called the Dress Game. It involved one of them putting a blanket around his waist like a skirt while the others tried to rip it off. I hated it and explained my feelings that it exemplified aggression against women and was just offensive. I can't say I always succeeded in my attempts to turn them to other endeavors, but at least they stopped doing it as they grew up, thank God.

And then there was the fighting. They couldn't keep their hands off each other. They were like puppies, always wrestling in a snarl of paws and tails. All their favorite shows featured fighting, like *Teenage Mutant Ninja Turtles*, which they wanted to watch multiple times per day. To wean them off it, Craig edited out all the fighting parts. The first time, oblivious, they watched the edited version, it just didn't have the same punch, and they slowly drifted away from the screen.

We were also externally challenged with gender stereotyping by the manufacturer of their favorite building toys, Legos. My boys liked the vacation-themed Lego sets, like Poolside Paradise, Seaside Cabana, and Island Arcade, but those were all in the pink aisle. I tried to be stealthy about it and get the sets out of the pink aisle before they could see that it was all "girl stuff." We wanted them to have Legos that fueled their imaginations and didn't want that stifled by gender boxes. But the company's marketing made it really hard.

The best we could do was be vigilant and call out things we saw that were sexist, not just sit there and let them slide. That kept us busy, because daily we witnessed parent–son interactions: "Boys don't cry" comments at the grocery store; "Let the poor little girl go first" at the playground; "No, you can't be a fairy—that's a girl costume" at the Halloween store. We did our utmost to convey our feelings and not encourage the sexist behaviors that our culture exposed them to, unfortunately.

We had some wins. When one of the boys, at seven years old, burst through the front door from school, saying, "Some people say I sing like a girl," he followed it with "I think that's a compliment. Not everyone can do that, you know." And one of my sons, of his own volition, was a fairy for Halloween one year.

DESPITE ALL OUR efforts, things happened. Two of our sons were accused of sexual harassment. The events occurred in junior high, when each of them was twelve years old. Along with our conscious efforts to raise liberated boys, the way Craig and I reacted to these unforeseen incidents played a big part in cementing our teachings.

One fall day before soccer practice, my middle son, Troy, and two of his friends changed out of their school clothes into their sports gear in a public restroom by the local swimming pool and soccer fields. There was a women's bathroom next to the men's, and for several weeks girl and boy soccer players ran in and out of their respective bathrooms with various missing garments to tease each other. This day, a girl a little younger than the boys came out of the girls' room just as Troy dashed out in his boxer shorts, with his white soccer shirt pulled down over them, so it looked like he wasn't wearing any pants.

He yelled, "Hi!" and the girl burst out crying and rushed to her mother, waiting outside, who called the boys out.

"What jerks you are. That's not nice. Say you're sorry," the girl's mother said, and the boys apologized.

They skulked off to soccer practice, flustered by the girl's strong reaction but relieved that the incident and the scolding were behind them. However, a week later, with a grim face, their soccer coach motioned Troy and his friends over. The mother had called the head of the soccer club and demanded the boys' expulsion from the team. She had also contacted the leader of the Boy Scouts, since she knew that two of the boys, one of whom was Troy, were working toward their Eagle Scout awards and wanted them kicked out of the Scouts program.

I was out of town on a business trip when the local soccer association held the incident review, but Craig was there in the meeting room, along with the parents of the other accused boys, the young girl's parents, and the leaders of the soccer team and Boy Scouts. I heard about the arm waving and heated words exchanged as the adults tried to sort out behavior, intent, and appropriate punishment. The point was made that what happened with the no-pants showing was an ongoing game that both boys and girls participated in, and that it was supposedly in fun. The punishment requested—eviction from the team and from Boy Scouts—smacked of over-severity for the actual event that had occurred. The mother of the young girl was adamant, though, that this was serious, and her child had been traumatized. I can see how upset she might have been for her daughter, and probably partially for herself, especially if she had been harassed or bullied at some point in her life. But as I heard the description of the meeting, it sounded like the men in the room saw her as emotional and overreactive. I'm not so sure.

If I had been there, I'd have supported that mother. Even though some of the men said, "This incident is not that big a deal," it *was* a big deal for her and for her daughter, and women and girls have found these kinds of events momentous for eons. The semisexual teasing of girls needs to stop with the small things, right at the beginning, so it doesn't grow and twist into bigger, uglier harassment in later years.

To their credit, the soccer and Scouts associations took the girl's ordeal seriously. In the end, Troy and his friends survived the Boy Scouts ousting but received a harsh suspension from a significant portion of the soccer season, as well as restrictions on where they could physically enter and exit soccer events. Their teammates took notice, so it served as a lesson for other boys that I hope influenced them as they grew up.

Troy, for his part, knew he had crossed a line, though he wasn't sure how far or what it all meant. He learned that each individual can react differently to how we treat him or her—we just never know how someone will respond—and he got a lesson in self-preservation and consequences for unacceptable behavior. He agonized, "Mom, I'm horrified about being labeled a sexual predator. I'm only twelve years old! Is sexual harassment the same as sexual perversion? It seems like it's all the same, all awful, and none of it is who I want to be." We worked through the definitions. I know it was a world-changer for him, and he never again harassed a girl.

ANOTHER DAY, MY youngest son, Weston, and four of his friends, rowdy seventh-grade boys, were waiting for their ride home along a shaded, sheltered trail by the back of the schoolyard. Jeanette—a small girl who stood quietly, with downcast eyes, next to my son in PE class—passed by daily.

The boys had taken to calling out to her, "Hey, Jeanette, we love you," as she scooted past them. Jeanette focused her stare on the ground, clutched her backpack to her chest, and hurried on.

On this afternoon, Weston's friends dared him to hug her, so when she scurried by that day, he sprinted over, arms outstretched, to do the deed. Jeanette screamed and nearly fell as she bolted. My son realized her distress and started to go after her and apologize, but she was already down the path, out of sight. He decided they shouldn't ever bother her again.

The next day, the junior high school principal himself called him out of math class, as his classmates whispered, "Ooh, Weston, what did you do?"

Weston walked slowly to the office, wondering what it was all about. He sat across from the principal and Joy, a school employee and local mother, who acted as a witness to the conversation.

"What happened after school yesterday?" they asked.

Weston knew right away what they were talking about and started to explain. Joy raged at him, "You touched her, didn't you?" and even though he kept saying he hadn't, she insisted, "Yes, you did. And if it were my daughter, I would get a restraining order against you," until Weston started to cry.

Jeanette had told her mother, then her mother had called the school, and now there was Weston, sniffling in the principal's office while Joy shouted at him. As badly as it was going for Weston, I later had to think on Jeanette's behalf, *Good for her. I never would have told my mother about something like that.* My heart pounded a little harder as I realized how far we'd come if a young girl felt comfortable sharing something like this.

These incidents had me squinting through the microscope at both the male and female sides of sexual harassment: *Is it true? Did my boys do it? Or do girls/women lie and falsely accuse boys/men to defame or ruin them? Do I have a predilection for the girls because I'm a feminist, or am I lenient with the boys because they're my sons?* I oscillated in my head between the girl's experience, an instinct to defend my beloved sons, and what the truth might be.

When I asked myself whether Jeanette's mother's response was extreme, I decided it wasn't. Even though her complaint was against my son, whom I love, I don't think she exaggerated. Her daughter was upset, and the mother stood up for her. I discovered that she was a single mom, divorced, and had work and personal pressures in her life, so she had her reasons. Maybe she had been taunted by boys and had never gotten over it.

Did Jeanette overreact? No, not according to *Ellison v. Brady*, the 1991 case in which the court decided that the standard in sexual harassment cases must be defined by the perspective of a "reasonable woman," not a "reasonable person." I told my boys, "Even though you think it was all fun in your minds, males and females might see things differently; behavior you find acceptable may offend girls. Girls are the majority of victims of harassment and rape, so they have a different level of fear and threat of violence than you might. You don't know how someone is going to react, so you have to be careful. And, by the way, you should know that the official definition of sexual harassment is 'unwelcome sexual advances . . . and other verbal or physical conduct of a sexual nature.' You did it, and the girls didn't like it."

I also related to the girl, to being alone and quiet and frightened and embarrassed. I never liked feeling that way, but in my day, we just took it and went home, cried into our pillows, and felt bad about ourselves. Some would say Weston and his friends just exhibited typical, culturally acceptable boy behavior. I sympathized with Weston, and I believed him when he said he hadn't touched her, but the incident reinforced to him that he wouldn't do anything like that ever again.

The principal called me on the phone at work, and we officially put the matter to bed by agreeing that Weston would write an apology to Jeanette and her mother. Later at home that night, I helped him write the letter. That act gave a scrap of resolution to Weston and me and, I hoped, to Jeanette and her mother as well, in my mental image of them sitting side by side at home on their couch, reading our symbol of admission and remorse.

BELIEVE ME, I didn't want my sons unduly punished. Accusations such as these can, and have, shattered young men's whole worlds. I certainly didn't want it shouted all over town that they were rapists. But sometimes things need to swing too far one way in order for societal change to be realized, even if boys suffer along the way. I'm glad these incidents happened when my sons were young, not older, when more severe consequences could have wrecked their lives.

Today, my boys don't harass women. I see them treating both women and men as individuals, with equal respect. "I'm meeting a friend for a workout," they say, and I don't know whether it's a male or female companion. My boys don't need their gender and its stereotyping to prop up their self-confidence, just as I hoped. One son rocked a pink umbrella to shelter us when it rained. Another sleeps on panda sheets for fun. My eldest kisses his three-year-old son every day. My sons bond with women—smart, kind, dedicated, who demand the same—in relationships balanced with mutual provision and dependence.

But even though they're now grown men, I'm not finished enlightening them. They learn my attitudes about current topics, such as #MeToo (love it) and the trend toward masculinization of women in films and gaming (hate it).

We have this conversation: "Mom, we know you don't like movies without any major female roles in them. You want to go see that new action movie? It has a woman as the main rebel warrior."

"Thanks for inviting me, but no way. All the producers of that film have done is make a man movie but put a woman in the same macho role. We don't need women becoming more like men, playing violent, aggressive parts and flinging around their AK-47s. We need movies where everyone can exhibit mature ways to work through problems and talk about what's going on, not engage in physical fighting. I know these don't make for blockbusters, but my kind of movies would be better for the human race."

LEGAL AND SOCIAL VALUES FOR THE NEXT GENERATION

RAISING LIBERATED BOYS is a fairly new topic in the United States. The women's liberation movement that began in the 1960s and carried on into the 1980s focused mainly on power and rights for women and girls, and feminism has been said to "ignore boys and young males." [1] Much of our history has involved going along with the culture of "be a man" and "don't make a girl out of him" and "boys don't cry." We women, as the primary child caregivers, need to institute change and incorporate the strength to buck our country's damaging masculine history. To me, raising enlightened boys is critical to stopping sexual harassment.

The rights of boys to live as more emotionally whole emerged in the 1990s, with Olga Silverstein and Beth Rashbaum's breakthrough book, *The Courage to Raise Good Men.* I support their statement that women need to have the confidence to stop being "collusive in this enterprise of 'toughening up' boys, as they try to get their sons to live up to their husbands' expectations (and their own)." [2] Women need to stand strong and stop perpetuating a "gender split" in which boys must achieve and girls must relate. Too often, we teach boys to shut down emotionally, as well as to take on the role of a "little man," in which his strength comes by virtue of not being feminine, with a lack of sentiment and empathy.

Silverstein and Rashbaum contend that male fear of femininity leads to an increase in "gender antagonism," in which young men view success and power as masculine and see women as objects of contempt, anger, lust, rape—and, I would add, sexual harassment.

Similarly, bell hooks stated in 2004, "Today small boys and young men are daily inundated with a poisonous pedagogy that supports male violence and male domination, that teaches boys that unchecked violence is acceptable, that teaches them to disrespect and hate women." [3]

More recently, in the 2010s, articles, books, and films have allotted more attention to raising boys with the self-confidence and empathy not to harass women. [4, 5, 6] But we have a long way to go. Today, I still see an emphasis on transforming girls into warriors, rather than on molding boys into emotionally connected beings. The current message is "Make our girls tough, but don't make our boys sensitive."

It's not that hard to raise strong girls and liberated boys. We should not be stereotyping either gender, according to Christia Spears Brown, who makes the data-based argument in her 2014 book, *Parenting Beyond Pink and Blue*, that boys and girls are so similar that we can't predict a child's emotional and physical aptitude based on his or her gender. She says, "For most traits and abilities, boys differ from other boys and girls differ from other girls more than the two groups differ from each other. Just because we like to ignore the variation within a group of boys or a group of girls doesn't mean it doesn't exist."[7]

eight

~⊃

THE CYCLE OF HARASSMENT

AS THE 2010S CAME INTO VIEW, MANY AMERICANS, including me, hoped that the social and political momentum Barack Obama ushered in during his eight-year presidency would bode well for continued gender and racial equality. By 2016, Hillary Clinton had emerged as such a strong contender as Obama's successor that the second half of the decade looked full of promise. As the election results rolled in state by state that November, my stomach ached from the kick in the gut, but I wasn't surprised. I thought, *Well, I had a slim hope that a woman would be president in my lifetime, but this is the way it's always been and confirms everything I've observed and experienced. A qualified woman is not as good as an unqualified man, and the man always gets the high-ranking job.* I recalled executive women leaving corporate America one after the other, my few role models gone, because they knew they would never get the top posts. We used to joke about how those positions went to tall white men with full heads of hair who played golf.

Not only would we not have a woman president in 2016, but the additional, cruel trick that set my head spinning was that America elected a sexual harasser as president. At the end of that year, twenty women had officially reported on the record that Donald J. Trump had sexually harassed them; twelve of these are accounts of physical assault. Credible women, such as Natasha Stoynoff, a writer for *People* magazine; Jessica Leeds, an American businesswoman; and Temple Taggart, who represented Utah at the 1997 Miss USA pageant, all gave detailed descriptions of Trump's unwelcomed sexual advances. Summer Zervos, a businesswoman and former *Apprentice* contestant, lodged a civil suit alleging that Trump forcibly kissed her, groped her breasts, and "thrust his genitals at her" in 2007. Trump denied all charges and called the women liars, even when he was caught on video bragging to radio and television host Billy Bush about how he can "grab them by the pussy," and if a man is famous, like he is, he can get away with it. A poll of registered voters of both Republicans and Democrats reported that 76 percent believe that Trump sexually harassed or assaulted women [1], but all this has now been swept under the sunburst-patterned Oval Office rug.

I kicked the floor, scrunched up my fists and face in an adult tantrum, called all my girlfriends, and marched in every women's protest I could when I realized the message from the 2016 election was that men had received permission to harass women. *So this is how it continues to be*, I thought. *Unbelievable. Even though sexual harassment is against the law, and a man admits to it on tape, as Trump did, it won't hurt his career at all—he can still be our country's leader. I can't imagine any other crime that someone confesses to on a recording, besides sexual harassment, that isn't at least investigated. He should be convicted, not rewarded with the presidency.*

The election also confirmed that old-boy cultural defenses still work—Trump labeled his comments simply "locker room talk" and thus excusable, allowing that powerful men are entitled to taking certain liberties with less powerful underlings. This incident said to America that we don't need to change our culture—the current one works just fine for most white males. It also sent women the message that if we do protest, our harassers will call us liars and nothing will be done about it, so we might as well be quiet and accept our role as victims. So far, our cultural norms have trumped the law and allowed our current president to practice harassment legally.

Sexual harassment in the workplace is far from over. Famous men are getting caught now, so we know it's still out there: Bill Cosby, Bill O'Reilly, Roger Ailes, Harvey Weinstein, Louis C.K., Roy Moore. And it's taking them down hard and by surprise. Ailes, chairman and CEO of Fox News, imagined himself invincible and denied the claims until he died, but he was finally stripped of his power by women in his own company, who sued him for propositioning and fondling them.

I watched the case against comedian Bill Cosby blare on TV for months in 2017, thinking, *The evidence is overwhelmingly against him. This is going to be a slam dunk. He admitted to giving quaaludes to women so he could have sex with them. Sixty women have accused him of sexually assaulting them, beginning back in the 1960s.*

I clenched my jaw and suppressed my urge to scream at the screen as I saw the woman who brought the case against Cosby, Andrea Constand—who considered Cosby a mentor for her work at Temple University as director of operations for the women's basketball team—treated like a criminal and called a liar and celebrity-seeker, just like Anita Hill and so many others. When the jury deliberated for days and then the case ended in a mistrial, I thought, *Oh my God, what does it take?*

The only good result from this situation was that some states lengthened the statute of limitations for rape, sexual assault, and sexual abuse from an average of ten years to twenty.

The previous limitation prevented legal consideration of the claims by other women against Cosby since the crimes had happened more than ten years earlier. It frequently takes a victim at least that long to rehabilitate, muster the strength and courage to reopen the wound she'd sooner keep bandaged up, find an opportunity for effective recourse, and speak up about the events.

Like the stereotypic light bulb joke, when Cosby finally got convicted in 2018, I thought, *How many women and how long does it take to convict one man of sexual assault? The answer, of course, is that it takes at least sixty women and fifty years.*

The cases against American film producer Harvey Weinstein counteracted the argument that men habitually make—that women falsely accuse them in order to gain wealth and fame. The fifty-eight women describing their sexual assault by Weinstein, among them Angelina Jolie, Gwyneth Paltrow, and Daryl Hannah, are already rich and famous. They had no incentive to lie. Similarly, Summer Zervos is suing Trump for only $3,000 to make the point that her complaint is not financially motivated.

The allegations against Weinstein launched the "Weinstein effect," where victims began speaking out about their sexual harassment from famous and powerful men. The Me Too movement, founded in 2006 by Tarana Burke, blew up as the #MeToo hashtag with an October 15, 2017, tweet by actress Alyssa Milano urging women and men to share their sexual harassment and assault stories through social media. This educated the public about how prevalent the problem was when Facebook reported twelve million posts on the topic within twenty-four hours of Milano's tweet. Twitter confirmed that more than 1.7 million tweets from eighty-five countries appeared with the hashtag in a little over a week. [2]

The situation with Roy Moore, the Republican candidate for Senate in Alabama, accused of harassing and molesting underage girls, had important ramifications because it cost the Republicans a Senate seat. It was one of the first times I have seen other men not rallying around to protect their kind. Some politicians distanced themselves from Moore, hinting at a new, hopeful break in the cycle of men supporting other men's denials of sexual harassment. A few men even spoke up and said they had witnessed Roy's penchant for young girls. Unfortunately, these accusations and his election loss did not lead to further investigation of his key supporter, Donald Trump, our harasser in chief.

Comedian Louis C.K. is the first powerful man I am aware of who admitted he sexually harassed the women who accused him. Most newsworthy men named as harassers categorically deny it. There are mixed views today about whom to believe, and a strong backlash and accusations of false allegations persist as means of mudslinging against women who accuse men of sexual harassment. Even some of our own sisters still choose to believe the men. In a 2018 survey, both a third of the men and a third of the women interviewed thought it was problematic that women manufacture claims of sexual harassment. [3]

There is more disbelief directed at the victims of sexual harassment crimes than in any other crime I know of today. I play this scenario in my head: *A man tells us someone stole his car. Do 33 percent of us automatically assume that the victim is making that up to get attention, or that he's accusing someone of the theft in order to settle a score with him? When the accused says, "I didn't do it," do we believe him and dismiss it as a "he said, he said"? Further, do we think of the victim,* Well, it's your own fault for driving a flashy red Porsche?

I believe the women. First, sound science supports the findings that only between 2 and 10 percent of sexual harassment reports are fabricated. [4, 5] As I have done throughout this book, my scientific training compels me to quote only data obtained through solid studies, with controls, statistical analysis, and adequate sample size, so I find this percentage to be accurately proven. Determining what is a false allegation and what is not is a tricky business, but most studies conclude that false allegations of sexual assault and harassment are highly overidentified by prosecutors and police (about 28 percent), because of practices heavily cemented in our culture. [6, 7] False reports are a popular but inaccurate perception, a bitch hunt. I go with the odds that there is a 90–98 percent chance the woman is telling the truth.

Of course, we all know people who lie, and some of us have been accused of crimes we didn't commit. Just like when my boss Lonnie alleged that I had cheated on my expense report—no small claim, because in the corporate world, if he could have proven it, it would have meant my immediate dismissal. And just as my manager Dr. Tim Johnson spread the lie that I was having an affair—an accusation that could have ruined my marriage. So, yes, there are bad people out there who seek revenge and possibly money or whatever else motivates liars, but it's noteworthy that the number of false sexual harassment reports is smaller than that of other crimes, such as thefts and burglary, phony accusations of which are a popular way to support insurance claims. [8, 9]

In addition to solid research findings that false accusations are low, the second reason I believe the women is that lying has so many negatives. The downsides (that you'd have to go through the wringer to prove it, you'd be called a liar and a whore, your reputation would be smeared, and you'd likely be retaliated against) are pretty certain and undesirable, while the upsides (that you'd actually win your case and get money and revenge) are unlikely. Additionally, it's at least a misdemeanor to provide a false report to law enforcement, so you could face jail time and payment of punitive and compensation damages if the alleged attacker decided to counter your claim. Women are speaking up not to profit from an elaborate lie or to randomly strike out at or falsely accuse men, but because we are compelled to right a wrong and achieve closure on something that has been haunting us for years.

Women are held up to incredible scrutiny in the few sexual harassment cases that actually get reported and investigated. In the 2010s, their allegations, intensely reviewed, were increasingly found credible and they began winning a number of those cases against major corporations. The financial services company UBS was found guilty and paid $10.6 million in 2011 to an employee whose supervisor made recurring remarks about her breast size and asked about her sexual fantasies. She was fired after she complained about it, even though UBS said it prohibits retaliation. In a drawn-out case in 2014, Chipotle Mexican restaurant in Houston compensated a sixteen-year-old girl whose supervisor harassed her. Chipotle claimed that the girl welcomed the sexual advances, even though Texas law declares that those under the age of seventeen cannot consent to sexual activity. And in 2016, former Fox News anchor Gretchen Carlson sued her boss, Roger Ailes, for on-the-job sexual harassment. She received $20 million and an apology from Fox.

Given these victories for women working for long-standing corporations, you might think that the tech startups so prevalent in the 2010s would be well equipped to nip in the bud even the slightest indication of sexism and harassment.

But I've been disappointed to realize that's not how it's stacking up in the younger tech industry. I pictured tech startups as opportunities for women to participate in cutting-edge, fresh enterprises, but the number of women in computer science has actually decreased in the last few decades. A high point was reached in 1984, when women earned almost 40 percent of computer science degrees. By 2018, that number had dropped to just 22 percent. [10] In 1990, women held 35 percent of computer and math jobs, but by 2013, their representation had been reduced to 26 percent. The percentage of women was even lower in other STEM fields in the workplace in 2016: 10 percent of electrical and computer hardware engineers, 8 percent of mechanical engineers, 11 percent of physicists. [11]

My sister, friends, and I couldn't wait for the old, sexist white men whom we'd had to deal with in past decades to die off so that we could bury or cremate their sexual harassment and discrimination right along with them. But younger men in the tech industry can be just as sexist, and women are sounding off about it. Dozens of women across the technology industry are talking about their sexual harassment experiences, actually naming harassers and showing evidence via emails and messages. They have called out Justin Caldbeck of Binary Capital, Dave McClure of 500 Startups, Chris Sacca of Lowercase Capital, and Marc Canter of Macromedia, to name a few. Uber admitted to the need for a full culture change after CEO Travis Kalanick went on "leave" in 2017, and both the number two guy, Emil Michael, and board member David Bonderman resigned—all for sexist remarks and behaviors. The company fired twenty workers following an investigation that substantiated reports of sexual harassment and began undergoing a "workplace culture" revamp. Kudos to Susan Fowler for exposing the behavior that started the scrutiny into Uber.

Tech has been described as a frat culture where the men are having fun in their boy world and want to keep it all for themselves, no girls allowed. Women see this exclusive culture, have a bad experience, and leave. The pervasiveness of sexual harassment and discrimination in tech explains to me why there are so few women in this industry.

I'm discouraged to read women's detailed accounts of their harassment experiences today and realize how similar their stories are to mine. In 2005, University of California, Berkeley, professor Geoff Marcy harassed Sarah Ballard, much like my professor did to me almost twenty-five years earlier. Ellen Pao describes sexual innuendos, aggression, and exclusion at the venture capital firm Kleiner Perkins that are similar to what I experienced. She recounts the same fear of reporting, the threat of reputation smearing, attacks, and retaliations that I swallowed in 1976.

It was September 27, 2018, but it could have been October 11, 1991, for me. This time, I wasn't ironing in my underwear on a business trip while I watched Anita Hill on TV. Now retired, I perched on my red cushioned chair in my home office, staring at my cell phone while Dr. Christine Blasey Ford also testified before the Senate Judiciary Committee about a Supreme Court nominee, this time Brett Kavanaugh, on the same subject: men's sexual behavior toward women. In this case, Ford accused Kavanaugh of sexual assault when they were both in high school. What I saw was the same wall of white men, the same skewering of a woman by men, the same struggle as fearful white men scramble to hold on to their power.

It shook me to the core. I had to pause the footage, stumble out of my chair to the nearby sliding glass doors, and gasp for air outside on our wooden deck overlooking my husband's retirement-project hydroponic garden. I sat down on an outdoor footstool, gripped with anxiety and trembling from my curly head to my bare toes.

Twenty-seven years later, we were in a time warp. The main takeaway points for me were twofold: One, we women must constantly be on the lookout for backlash—men trying to find extreme cases of sexual harassment and assault to try to detract from and discredit the #MeToo movement. Instead of focusing on the accusation that Brett Kavanaugh lied under oath in 2006 while testifying about his role in the 2002 nomination of Judge Charles Pickering, here we were, debating whether or not what someone does in high school matters and whether women lie. I believe these power-hungry white men preferred to take on a case they believed a lot of the public would support, a case about which the average citizen might comment, "Gee, I did a lot of things in high school, too, boys will definitely be boys. This #MeToo thing has gone too far. Enough already! Men have rights!" It's easier to focus on something entertaining and not so cut-and-dried as lying under oath, something that still asks the perpetual question "Do we believe women? Aren't most of them making this up?"

My second takeaway from the Ford-Kavanaugh testimony, especially after he was (of course) confirmed as a Supreme Court justice, is that we women need to very carefully prepare and arm ourselves to continue the sexism battle for years and years to come.

It's incredible that even women who have become power figures themselves in more recent years are still subject to harassment from men. We may think that if women had more power, harassment would stop. But it doesn't work that way. Even if we are in the superior position, men in inferior positions will still harass us. A prominent dentist friend of mine recounted that after she'd completed her dental work on an eighty-year-old man, he asked, "Can I thank you by giving you a hug?"

"Well, um, all right," she said reluctantly, trying to be a good sport.

But then, as he hugged her, he moved his head and kissed her on the lips and stuck his tongue in her mouth.

"Oh my God," she related to me. "My assistant saw the whole thing, and we were both mortified. It ruined my day, and hers, too. When I finally went home, I cried at the anger and shame of it all."

I thought, *Harassment can still happen when the power dynamic is reversed, even when the man is in a subjugated position and the woman has full and easy access to a dental drill.*

In 2017, the musician Taylor Swift was grabbed on the ass by a male fan who lifted up her skirt during a photo shoot. How could he have been so bold as to do that to a renowned figure like Swift? He relied on the historical right of men to attack women, rather than taking the current power dynamics into account. Congratulations to Swift for suing him for sexual assault (for $1, again to make the point that this is not all about money), in solidarity with other women in the rampantly sexist music business. But it saddens me that, in spite of all of women's current advancements, old beliefs and habits still die hard.

Not only has sexual harassment not been purged from the workplace, but it's now actually expanded to the Internet. Since it's not well regulated, harassers have an open, new medium for their evil deeds, and young women are particularly targeted. According to recent studies, young women experience severe physical threats and ongoing harassment that lead to long-term impacts, such as emotional tolls, career disruption, and damage to their reputations. [12] The Wikimedia

Foundation is launching an initiative to address harassment on Wikipedia and other Wikimedia projects through new tools, more stringent policies, and the employment of volunteers to quickly identify harassing behavior, evaluate harassment reports, and respond quickly. But we need more. The old principles of degrading and threatening women have just moved to a modern forum.

So, given all this, what can we do about it? To relieve our society and women of this soul-crushing, demeaning behavior, we need to break the whole circular chain of our culture. This chain consists of several links, from early parenting to schools and universities to corporations. There are ways to do this, and it's not rocket science.

Overall, we can together support a movement for boys' and men's liberation (BAML) to enable them to experience complete emotional lives and equality. Many "angry white men" in America today believe they are "entitled" yet "disempowered by feminism" and take their hostilities out on women. [13] To address this anger, they require a new definition of masculinity, a "democratic manhood" that is "an egalitarian manhood, accepting and even embracing the equality of the women in our lives, and preparing our children for the lives they will surely live of greater gender and sexual equality." [14] BAML must include boys (hence the name), not just adult men, in order for us to start early, with a new generation of males.

We also need a leader for BAML, a Gloria Steinem, but for boys and men. A job description for this position might read:

"The leader of the Boys' and Men's Liberation Movement (BAML) will inspire boys and men to forge a cultural shift that allows them to lead fuller lives. This will be accomplished by creating the following for boys and men: evolved gender roles, diverse opportunities in society as fit interests and skills, wider job and role prospects, full engagement in family life and relationships for working fathers and career men, an expanded definition of worth beyond success, a clear path for raising liberated boys, and a program of admiration and respect for women. The leader will strive to free boys and men from the narrow definitions of masculinity, the burden of sole breadwinner, the barriers of anger and isolation, restricted patriarchal bonds, and oppression by which they are enslaved to their jobs, isolated from their families, and emotionally shut down. The leader will be relatable to males of both conventional and liberated masculinity, in order to unite all men. An outstanding leader will possess strong communication, emotional, and personal skills and will open the way for men to live as full human beings. The leader will embolden men and boys to maintain liberated, emotionally plentiful lives as partners, fathers, friends, lovers, and parents."

I want to see someone step forward.

We once had a men's liberation movement in the United States. It sprang up among heterosexual, middle-class men in the 1960s and '70s, as a response to the feminist movement, and focused on the negative stereotypes of traditional male roles. Men's discussion groups abounded in the '70s. Warren Farrell formed the National Task Force on the Masculine Mystique within the National Organization for Women in 1971. Farrell holds the title as the "intellectual father of the men's rights movement" today. [15] He currently chairs a commission to create a White House Council on Boys and Men, but I'm sure that's struggling under the current administration. Consciousness-raising groups, men's centers, books, and conferences popped up around America throughout the 1970s. Sadly, by the late 1970s, the movement sputtered out.

Far-right males founded antifeminist men's rights group, while liberal-leaning men attached themselves to the feminist movement.

We need BAML to replace the men's liberation movement that died, as well as other actions, to eliminate sexual torment. Here's how each segment of the chain of sexual harassment—parents, schools, and corporations—can help:

Parents: The key to a better future, in my opinion, is infusing our boys with self-assurance and sensitivity through conscientious parenting. With inner confidence, boys won't harass and bully girls, because they won't have to do it to make themselves powerful. Our culture sadly lacks liberated boys, which is why I've devoted a whole chapter to how to raise them.

I feel sorry for men, in that they are taught as children not to cry or express their emotions, to hold them in. But we can change this by bringing up our boy children to embrace both traditionally feminine and masculine qualities. BAML can help with this. I also call women to action: "You, as the main child raisers in today's culture, have the perfect opportunity to make liberated men the new reality by instilling the right values in your boys. Do it."

I'd like to see Eliza Doolittle in *My Fair Lady* singing "Why Can't a Man Be More Like a Woman?" to Professor Henry Higgins. Instead of masculinizing girls to show their power and strength, we parents also need to spend time feminizing boys (and girls) to grow their sensitivities and teamwork skills.

A blend of both power and sensitivity is the right formula for parents to transfuse into their children. I've always harkened back to Philip Wylie's 1951 book, *The Disappearance*, in which he creates two parallel worlds. One afternoon, all the men disappear, leaving a world of women, while in another world, all the women vanish, leaving a world of men. The man world—violent, over-sexualized, aggressive, and warring—still runs because men in business and government previously created and dominated it. The woman world has social stability—it learns how to reproduce, and peace reigns—but technically it regresses because so few women have been trained in technology, business, and government. This world can't train enough women fast enough. They're fully capable, but men have beaten them down and misshapen them to such an extent that they're now unable to perform because of low self-esteem. I'd like to see BAML offering a mix of these two worlds, one that emphasizes the qualities in the women's world, because it's more peaceable, but also fully realizes the benefits of interconnection between the qualities of the two sexes.

I've often wished I had been born a boy. I would love to see a boy Lucinda and compare him today with the girl Lucinda, to see how life turned out for him. I believe that the boy Lucinda would have had more prospects and gone further professionally. But we can fix that today by raising boys and girls who represent both sides of the spectrum. A boy or girl raised with encouragement, support, love, and opportunities is the best possible combination you can get.

As for girls: Parents need to start early with positive messages for them. Tell them they're capable in STEM fields—don't drive them away from science and math by playing to their insecurities and discouraging them. Help them choose the classes and goals they want in elementary through high school, especially if those goals are traditionally male. Use the resources available today: nonsexist toys; the new, all-inclusive Scouts BSA program; all-gender tech camps. Build their self-esteem by teaching them to believe in themselves so that they will not end up as young, fearful women. Give them the confidence to slug it out when they need to.

The whole confidence thing critically impacts how a woman deals with sexual harassment, so parents must focus on teaching that certitude to their girls. I still get angry and envious when I read about confident women who had supportive parents, especially fathers, and talk about being tough (Barbara Boxer) and just leaning in (Sheryl Sandberg).

Yes, I'm envious. How do you lean in and act tough if you weren't taught self-confidence early? It's not that easy. In her autobiography, Barbara Boxer talks about how her parents "taught [her] to face problems and challenges with values, beliefs, and a sense of purpose." [16]

Hillary Clinton related that her father was just as supportive of her aspirations as he was of her brothers'. She recalled that her parents "treated my brothers, Hugh and Tony, and me like three individual kids, with three individual personalities, instead of putting me in a box marked 'female' and them in a box marked 'male.' They never admonished me for 'not acting like a girl' when I played baseball with the boys. . . . [T]hey didn't want their daughter to feel constrained by tired ideas of what women should do with our lives. They wanted more for me than that." [17]

"My father was a feminist from the day I was born, and there was nothing he thought his little girl couldn't do," Condoleezza Rice remarked. [18]

Sheryl Sandberg said, "I was raised to believe that girls could do anything boys could do and that all career paths were open to me." [19]

Former Miss America and news anchor Gretchen Carlson said she was "raised in an era in which I was told nothing could hold me back. It didn't enter my mind that my gender was an obstacle. I was determined to be bold and make my mark." [20]

Even in the 1950s, other households were different from mine, in that some fathers were around more. One time a friend, who often came to my house, saw my father sitting on the couch and said, "Who's that?"

I saw other fathers spending time with their daughters, attending parent-teacher conferences, showing up at recitals, and attending father–daughter dinners. I heard other fathers saying, "Good job!" to their daughters when they showed them a well-received school paper, while I never got that. I saw other girls getting attention and gifts from their fathers and wondered why I didn't get that kind of love from mine.

My parents taught me to shut up, stay in the background, cower at problems, lie low, give up, and especially not stand up for myself. Because of these lessons, I learned how to revel in the hurt that I got from harassment and saw myself as a pathetic victim with no recourse. So, all I can say to Barbara, Hillary, Condoleezza, Sheryl, and Gretchen is, you are so lucky.

It's light-years easier to be a strong woman if you were encouraged and respected as a child. And a girl with self-regard can stand up to her harassers more readily. So let's all work consciously to instill self-esteem in our girls.

Schools and Universities: Our educational systems can be part of the efforts of BAML. We can work early in the lower grades with parents to reinforce teaching sensitivity, non-bullying, and inclusion. Educators, particularly guidance counselors, should be trained to help boys explore their full range of emotions—even those considered "not masculine," like fear, shame, humiliation, and uncertainty. I've always believed we need more male teachers who can stand as strong and sensitive male role models. Females dominated our American school setting in 2017, all the way from preschool and kindergarten (98 percent female) up to elementary and middle school (79 percent) and high school (59 percent). [21] This situation smacks of even less diversity than the white-male-dominated corporations that we're fighting to change. Increased diversity in our teaching staffs would better serve our mixed population of boys and girls and ensure that all their interests, whether masculine- or feminine-leaning, are recognized. School officials must ask themselves, "In what ways am I being sexist in my treatment of boys? Am I disapproving of boys' interests in our classrooms? Am I keeping traditionally female fields open to them in high school and college?"

When I attempted to hire an executive administrative assistant, a key position on my staff, no males applied and I couldn't locate even one. We need more men in fields where women represented, in 2014, 75 percent or more of the total employed: dental hygienists, nurses, human resources managers, hairstylists, occupational therapists, paralegals, librarians, dieticians, special education teachers, and so on. [22] A primary driver that keeps men out of these work arenas is, of course, money, since it's well documented that women are paid less than men—almost 20 percent less across all full-time workers, according to 2017 figures. [23] A man who can pocket $20 per hour as a welder isn't interested in "slumming" as a health care worker for $11. But another key factor in why men shy away from these jobs is cultural conditioning that is deeply ingrained from a young age. Faced with the unfortunate historical term "pink-collar jobs," men view these positions as lower-status "women's work" and skirt whole fields to avoid association with empathetic, caring helper roles in order to seek what they perceive as masculine, tough jobs—sort of a "we want to build things, not take care of people" mentality.

This cultural bias exists even in the face of data showing that "female" vocations, such as health care, are the fastest-growing job segments, while traditionally "masculine" jobs, like steelworking, are declining, and that men who enter female-dominated professions are promoted faster than their female colleagues—the new "glass elevator." [24, 25]

As well as fighting this cultural bias by encouraging boys to investigate conventionally female careers, our educators must advocate traditionally male fields for girls all along the academic journey. Girls already draw unwanted attention if they choose typically masculine classes or majors in college. A young university woman I talked to said to me, "One hundred percent of the girls in my engineering class are named Sara." There were only two of them, both named Sara. Let's not make it worse for them by favoring boys and maintaining an uncomfortable macho atmosphere.

Girls did not start entering STEM classes in large numbers until the 1990s, but by 2017, about half the students in high school math and science courses were girls. They score almost identically to boys on standardized tests, so they are more than capable and competitive in these fields. However, 2018 data showed that, although we have 50 percent girls in STEM fields in high school, that number shrinks to 24–37 percent in college, and then again to 8–26 percent in the workplace. [26]

Unfortunately, "a widespread culture of sexual harassment drives women away from science careers and perpetuates a gender gap." [27] A 2018 report by the National Academies of Sciences, Engineering, and Medicine revealed that in high school through graduate school, young women experience, see, hear about, or read about sexual harassment in STEM fields and companies and then change their major, quit, or decide not to pursue STEM studies. [28] The report concludes that "indirect experiences" can be just as powerful as personally experiencing sexual harassment and that active "whisper networks" warn women away from certain paths. In classrooms and at conferences and job fairs, young women sometimes took me aside after the formal remarks and furtively asked, "What's it really like being the only woman on your team?"

I had to answer honestly, admittedly as a part of the whisper network, "It's tough. You will face discrimination and harassment because you are a woman. You will sometimes feel very alone. It's manageable, and you can have an amazing career. We need you to enter STEM fields to change this modus operandi, but I'm not going to lie—you will need a support system to get through it."

We pay a high price when our young women who did well in high school STEM fields elect not to pursue them into college and the workplace because of fears of sexual harassment and exclusion. Diversity in STEM brings new ways to view an issue, manage a team, solve a problem. These skills will all be lost for girls unless trends change.

Universities are taking a few steps in the right direction. Actions to combat sexual harassment include screening and hiring nonsexist teachers, providing sound harassment training, and continuing to punish faculty members for sexual harassment offenses. The nonprofit organization Callisto developed a confidential online tool that allows students to report sexual harassment more easily and confidentially. The tool contains a novel matching system to uncover repeat offenders. Since 2016, more than a dozen universities have deployed Callisto.

Australia, Ireland, and the United Kingdom utilize a program called Athena Scientific Women's Academic Network

(SWAN), funded by their governments, to recognize gender equality achievements in academia. Started in 2005, SWAN initially focused solely on STEM fields, but in 2015 it expanded to include law, business, art, and social science departments. The program has gold-, silver-, and bronze-level awards for institutions that release and explain all their data on gender equality in the areas of pay, grade levels, contracts, dropout rates, job offers, promotions, acceptance rates, and policies at all levels of their organizations. A 2017 study of SWAN's effectiveness showed that the program has had an impact on advancing gender equality by, for example, addressing unequal representation of women and offering flexible work schedules to both men and women.

In the United States, the National Science Foundation is funding a project called STEM Equity Achievement (SEA) Change to enact cultural reconstruction in public and private higher-education institutions. The project, a partnership between universities and the American Association for the Advancement of Science, assesses schools' commitment to promoting an equal, safe environment for women and minorities in STEM fields. The project developed a rating system similar to SWAN's to recognize schools that create a friendly culture for underrepresented groups. Ideally, institutions will see possessing this certification as a competitive advantage.

Our educational system has the job of providing a school-to-career pipeline so that corporations will have a good selection of diverse candidates to hire. They need to be sure women stay in technical fields by providing female-friendly, non-harassing environments. A girl should never have to fight off her teachers like I did.

Corporate America: Corporations must be a part of BAML. To advance their culture, companies can advocate for men who want to change the female–male dynamic. The 2017 Study of Women's Health Across the Nation found that, to spur gender equality, organizations need to execute wide structural, cultural, and policy changes to give men incentives to participate more in family life. This is a perceptive finding that can be applied in corporations where the plodding of the men's liberation movement is markedly exposed. Corporate policies can be adjusted to support men who want parental leave, time for child pickup/drop-off, and the opportunity to raise their kids and spend time with their families. We need to allow men to function as loving parents and embrace new parenting roles, and to reward them when they do so. Full-time fathers still face an unfair stigma, and no "daddy track" exists. This needs to change—we don't need a mommy or daddy track; we just need paid family leave, childcare, and a family-friendly workplace for both men and women.

Finding affordable childcare is stressful for all parents, yet corporations are staying away from it, which makes no sense, since they're already involved in medical and dental insurance, gym memberships, credit unions, and so many other parts of their employees' lives. Every company I worked for formed a study team of women to consider childcare as an employee benefit, including possible on-site daycare, child sick care, or reimbursement for single parents needing to hire overnight caregiving because of required work travel. I was asked repeatedly to be part of these teams, but I refused each time, explaining, "If I lead or sit on this committee, it only perpetuates the myth that only women have this issue, that women are the ones who have to figure out childcare. This is both a father *and* a mother conundrum, so we need a mixed team."

I knew that a team run by women was doomed in my male-dominated companies. Men, even if asked, declined to participate because they didn't want the perception that they weren't 100 percent devoted to their jobs—they would appear distracted, not full company men, if they fessed up that they, too, had to worry about childcare. These efforts all failed anyway, as the companies I worked for persisted in their belief that because this benefit was mostly for women, it wasn't that important and wouldn't serve all employees. However, by offering childcare, corporations can level the playing field for women and men.

One way I approached shifting the culture at work was by recruiting higher-level men to participate in the change, so that others would feel as if they had permission to do likewise. My highest-ranking male employee, Carl, was about to have a baby, and I told him, "Carl, you should really consider taking some time off when your child is born. It's a once-in-a-lifetime experience. Sadly, it's not a fully paid benefit in America— the only industrialized country in the world not to have paid parental leave, by the way—but you can at least apply for partial benefits."

Carl said, "I've actually never even considered it, but I'll go home and talk to my wife about it."

The next day, he entered my office and said, "My wife is really enthusiastic about your idea and told me to please send you her utmost thanks. I'm going to take personal leave."

Once Carl returned from a month off, he told others in the office what a wonderful adventure it had been to spend time with his baby. Then, when Ed was expecting a child, I asked Carl to go talk to him and encourage Ed to take time off, which he did, and then Ed came back from leave and raved about the experience, too. Then Ed told Thomas and Thomas went on baby leave, and so it went. Men are deprived of certain rich and meaningful experiences in life because of

American macho culture. All parents should get to spend time with their newborn.

Some men are now standing up and even taking parental-leave issues to court. In *Joshua Levs v. Time Warner*, Levs sued for more paternity leave for fathers, since men currently face ridicule and job backlash if they take paternity leave. They're seen as pussy-whipped if they take it at all, and if they do it, they're expected to take as little as possible and rush back to the office to prove how committed to work they are.

I heard Frederick brag, "I haven't taken any vacation this year—I'm just too busy!"

Bernard claimed, "I took vacation with my family but worked the whole time on the beach."

Brad said, "I missed my daughter's soccer team victory, but that's okay because we had our weekly meeting."

These concessions from men do not help change the workplace. We need men to be brave by demanding and then utilizing flexibility in their work lives. Doing so does not impact revenue—in fact, I believe it improves the bottom line. I blame US workaholic culture for holding back workplace evolution—our jobs are twenty-four/seven, and the more hours we work, the more self-sacrificing we appear and the more we're rewarded, even if none of this has much to do with results.

But backlash lurks in the corporate world for men who try liberation. One lovely spring day at work, I hosted a baby shower for one of my employees. Gathered in the large, open cafeteria with friends and colleagues, I stopped to chat with my employee's husband and asked him, "Is your division at work throwing a shower for you, too? I love to celebrate with baby showers for both men and women in my group."

He said, "Wow, no way. That would be seen as a waste of time. They don't encourage men's involvement in their families. If I took time off to pick up my daughter from daycare because she was sick, or if my wife were out of town on business and I had to keep regular hours because of the children, they would hassle me for not acting serious about my career."

He later quit to find a more family-friendly workplace. It's unfortunate that he didn't stay to help change his old company, but I swell with hope to see men taking a stand. Role sharing is a key aspect of developing empathy and reducing shopworn male–female behaviors and attitudes in the workplace.

For women, corporations must reverse the pervasive sexist culture so that women, instead of being repelled by the stories they hear through the whisper networks, will actually be attracted to certain companies as fair places to work. Women hear about the bad corporate culture that pervades STEM industries and decide early on in college not to go into computer science or whatever male-type field interests them, no matter what exciting, challenging opportunity may present itself.

Once women are hired into male-dominated workplaces, companies must make it their job to keep them there. Corporations can support programs that help both men and women, like childcare and flex time. They can set clear policies that safeguard women and make harassers understand that their misconduct has consequences. Companies must ensure a safe place for harassed individuals to report to—where those victims know they will be respected and heard, without retaliation.

We can expand university efforts, such as SWAN, SEA Change, and Callisto, to corporations. I would have had my department apply for and utilize these systems and tools if they'd been available. I would definitely have seen these tools as an advantage, as amazing women and minorities flocked to my group. I tried to have a woman- and minority-friendly organization anyway, but these approaches are a solid means of measuring and advertising it.

Corporations currently beg off accountability for their low numbers of women employees by saying that only 20 percent or less of bachelor's degrees in the sciences are awarded to women, so companies have only a small pool from which to choose. But corporate America has its responsibility, too, and management can change the culture. Though industries can't be condemned for their mostly male demographic, they also can't pin everything on the pipeline problem. Making their cultures more appealing to women will affect the majors that women select in college and will give corporations a larger pool from which to select female candidates.

I've had experience changing and building a safety culture in a large organization, and I see it as similar to building a culture free of sexual harassment and sexism. Set the vision at the top, make the leaders walk the talk, and keep everyone accountable. It can be done. When I worked in corporate safety, we set goals for zero safety incidents. With this method and loads of hard work, we reduced accidents and injuries and ensured that everyone went home safely. We can apply this model to sexual harassment and chop it down to zero incidents.

We had an expression in the safety culture, "If you see it, you own it." Everyone gets involved—if you see sexual harassment, you have a responsibility to speak up. Companies can utilize this "bystander intervention" as a powerful ax to curb bullying. All employees should be trained to know that they are required to act when they witness sexual harassment. Getting everyone involved and accountable will start the shift in the culture. Call out every single time someone says something sexist or off the mark, and teach everyone to support and reward that conduct.

In the construction and maintenance of an incident-free safety culture, repercussions against offenders must be clear, harsh, and quick. Rules such as driving without a seat belt or while intoxicated should be punishable by immediate dismissal. Everyone will know these rules and that if they're not followed, the consequences will be a NIC—negative, immediate, and certain. (In this case, you'd be fired.) In a reinforcement-based leadership style of management, PICs (positive, immediate, and certain) and NICs are powerful behavior modification tools available to managers. Both PICs and NICs can be applied to reinforce positive and discourage negative sexual behaviors.

A dramatic, albeit fictional, example of this concept pops up in Naomi Alderman's book *The Power*, in which young women are infused with the ability to cause unbearable pain with one touch. When used against sexual harassers, rapists, and the like, their touch stops offensive behavior. Since we don't have that, we could, for example, PIC those who exhibit bystander intervention with recognition and awards and NIC harassers with a disgraceful and public discharge.

Our current corporate sexual harassment training is ineffectual, since it puts the onus on the victim to end the harassment—a mind-boggling task for someone who feels weak, small, and bullied. We need to focus on the behavior of the harasser and those in a position of power to stop it. It has to be clear that harassing behavior is unacceptable and will be punished. We cannot continue to accept the ease with which men are capable of denying the charges—like former Fox News host Bill O'Reilly, who eschewed all the accusations against him while paying out hush money.

Unfortunately, employers can sidestep harassment suits by showing that they have policies and training programs in place, without having to prove whether or not the programs are effective. This work-around leads to training conducted more to avoid liability than to actually create change. Walmart has been plagued with sexual harassment cases since 1997. Even though it has an anti-sexual harassment policy and in-house training, evidence emerged that management didn't receive the training, and that the training and policy were not enforced. [29]

New training programs to change the culture also need to include education of employees, supervisors, and managers on the existence of laws and company policies. Too often, as was the case for me, there were laws in place that could have helped me, but I didn't know about them, and my company culture did not encourage me to learn more. Many of my workplaces offered good policies, like leave, job accommodations, and inclusion, but lax supervisors simply ignored them. All this needs to be included in employee and manager training, along with consequences to managers who choose not to deploy existing policies.

Creating a new female–male dynamic through programs, such as childcare and family leave, that benefit both men and women help remove behaviors like sexual harassment by reducing stereotypes and old roles. A reduction in sexual harassment at corporations will only increase productivity. Think of all the dollars lost in productivity if we add up the millions of hours women waste at work angsting over what the hell we're going to do about the latest sexual harassment incident. And it's not just the sufferer who worries—if there were onlookers, then coworkers are involved. If the victim reports the event, then the harasser and the supervisors of the harasser and victim become part of the expanding tableau.

I had one sexual harassment case as an executive that took

up weeks and weeks of my time, not to mention the cost to the company when the victim actually sued. Then there were more resources and time sucked up, along with lawsuit costs, fines, and settlement money. Not handled properly, a complaint triggers further workplace damages, like distraction, loss of productivity, and possible turnover. And if the harassment case becomes public, a company can face brand and reputation damages; then Public Affairs' job expands, requiring more time and resources. I applaud those companies that possess the smarts to realize the business ramifications and invest in and focus on the creation of harassment-free workplaces.

conclusion

∽

STAY AND SPEAK UP

WOMEN MUST STAY IN THE MAN WORLD AT UNIVERSITIES and in corporate America and speak up about the sexual harassment they face. I know staying is hard, but women must be in the soybean field, on the oil platform, and at the conference table to make a difference. They wanted me to go away, but I guess that was my victory—I kept coming back. Just show up the next day, hold your head high, and look them in the eye. Speak up about your opinions and about sexist behavior in order to heal and institute change.

I know it's a tough assignment to both work and be outspoken in male-dominated organizations. I know we might get fired, demoted, sidelined, or blackballed. We might get called a slut, ugly, a liar, a bitch. America's corporate culture of sexual harassment and discrimination against women and its "frat boy" mentality are unappealing to many young women, who say, "Screw it. I won't put up with that." I don't blame them.

So why stick it out?

If we women stay, exciting careers and a fighting chance to make an impact with large-scale projects await us. For me, inventing an environmentally safe herbicide, saving the California condors, helping rice farmers in Japan, restoring mangrove forests in Nigeria, and cleaning up contaminated properties across the world tipped the scales toward the positive. If we are part of a large operation that has substantial influence in the world, we can leverage that clout to make things happen. Wearing the badge of a big corporation or university gives us access to funding, people, boards of directors, and opportunities that are absent if we're with a small, unknown business. We can collaborate with smart colleagues and grow professionally in a challenging and global workplace—not to mention the financial gains we reap, since many corporations pay well and award bonuses, stock options, retirement savings programs, and other benefits.

Women add so much to corporations: They lower the ego level in the room, propose alternative ideas, bring a different perspective, understand the female market, demand fairer practices, and create financial benefit. Multiple studies from renowned research institutions and universities find a strong correlation between the presence of female leaders and a firm's increase in profitability, corporate performance, and earnings that outpace their industry's. [1, 2, 3] A significant part of growth in worker productivity in the United States between 1960 and 2008 resulted from the removal of barriers to women. [4] In a twelve-year study that wrapped up in 2014, the eighty women who led Fortune 1000 companies during that period delivered shareholder returns that were three times the S&P 500 index. [5]

The whole room, team, or meeting is off-kilter if no women are present. If we are there, we can raise viewpoints that might not be evident in a room full of masculine energy. We can encourage another woman, if she is there, to verbalize her thoughts—there is strength in any number over one. We can find and build allies among men who are sympathetic to our cause, so it's not just women alone. We can advocate for sustainability, values, wellbeing, collaboration, empathy, vision, innovation, and fairness. We can influence and change strategies, policies, and systems. We can fight against bullies who are in it just for themselves. By observing bad male bosses, we can switch things up and become great bosses—those who know that if we treat people well, we get more out of them. I found that if I gave my employees some slack to attend their daughter's school play, I was paid back in spades. They would push hard nights and weekends for me to meet a deadline if I asked them. If we encourage others' opinions and reward them when they contribute, we'll build a strong team that produces solid results because it's considered all the perspectives and twists and turns.

Still, many women leave, like I did a few times. That's how we make sexual harassment stop in our everyday lives—we get away from our harassers. Here are what I see as the options for women to lessen the impact of sexual harassment and sexism in our professional circumstances:

- Start our own companies.
- Find careers at woman-operated, female-friendly companies.
- Stay in a male-dominated company and slug it out.

I'm an advocate for all of the above and fully understand why women make these choices, but the last one on the list still resonates with me. I am here to say we can't keep leaving. Man-controlled corporate America is continuing without us, and that is where the power still sits—politically, economically, globally. And we can't keep giving the power to men—we hand it over to them if we don't participate. We can't let them have all the authority just because it's unpleasant to fight for it. We could all leave, but the male-operated companies would still rule. They've been around longer, and the men have it down. They control major, influential segments of our society, like energy, technology, manufacturing, and filmmaking.

After leaving jobs and workplaces to escape my harassers, only to find myself at other, equally male-dominated companies, I thought about transferring into a more "female" field or starting my own business—but then I had a chance to ask Gloria Steinem for advice.

At all those laborious leadership training sessions where they ask you, "Who is your hero?" and most of the men say, "My father" or "Thomas Jefferson," I always said, "Gloria Steinem."

The male participants usually asked, "Who's that?" and I sighed.

I met her at a conference. She was alone for a split second, so I went up to her and told her of my trials but added that I felt like working from the inside of a corporation had its purpose. Gloria listened closely, asked a few questions, and said, "I know there are a lot of other options, but if you can do it, you should stay." [6]

I know it sounds minor, but that little bit of encouragement made a gigantic difference for me. So I am giving that same advice to all of you women who are vacillating about quitting the man world: If you can do it, you should stay and become a champion of internal change.

ONCE INSIDE PREDOMINANTLY male organizations, women *must* advocate for other women. There are still so few of us in the corporate world that unification is imperative. It disgusts me to see women fighting among themselves. Often, I saw a successful woman unwilling to include other women. She wanted to be the only female figure around the refinery or at the wheat harvest and liked her exclusive status. Or she feared that supporting other women would get her kicked out of the men's club in which she had struggled so hard to gain membership. And others won't admit to ever having harassment or discrimination issues because it makes them look weak, or because they don't want to be a "problem." But we must unveil our secrets; it's the only way to bring the matter to mainstream attention. It's misguided to try to be the lone she-wolf. Women comprise more than 50 percent of the population in the United States, yet we remain complicit in our own bondage. If we were united, we could rule companies and the country.

And we must continue, no matter how tiresome it is, to call out discriminatory language, like "she's too pushy," while men with the same behaviors are seen as leaders. During employee promotions and evaluations, we have to be right at the grown-up table when men say, "She's a new mother and can't travel, so we shouldn't consider her for that higher-level job."

This is our opportunity to push back our chair, stand up, and say, "Did you ask her? Do you know she won't travel? Maybe she can't wait to travel and have time alone! Maybe her husband or her father takes care of the baby. You don't know—you're making huge gender generalizations." We must be in the room for the culture to change.

Learning to voice my opinions, risking being the only feminist in the office, helped me heal. I started with the easier stuff: not blasting gender inequities right out of the gate, but just figuring out how to get the floor. I watched how men did it. On work trips, I practiced in my hotel room, striding around in my nightgown, how to break into a discussion and be heard. I grew my vocal chords—they became stronger as I tried them out, and I had lots of opportunities to keep speaking when a man tried to interrupt me. I learned how to enter a conversation when the men would not stop talking. The first time it worked, when I kept my lips moving and my voice raised even though a man was trying to talk over me, I sucked in my breath in disbelief but just kept going, my confidence bubbling up in my chest. And then nothing bad happened. No one got mad at me. I wasn't rapped on the head with a spoon. In fact, I was able to finish my sentence and make my point.

The first five hundred times men stole my ideas in the meeting room, I let it slide. Then one day, after one of my recommendations had again been attributed to a man, even though I had just said it, I found my voice. "I'm so glad Dale took up the thread of my proposal. I figured it out last night and would like to tell all of you about it," I said.

If I knew another woman was attending the discussion, I made a pact with her ahead of the meeting time, so when the inevitable happened and a man got credit for our ideas, one of us spoke up and said, "I like that Dale is following up on the solution that Beth proposed to this group about fifteen minutes ago. Let's hear what she has to say. Great idea, Beth, by the way."

I floated above the meeting-room scene of coffee cups, strewn papers, open laptops, and crumpled muffin liners, beaming while thinking, *You go, girls!* Seeing it actually work, when the meeting facilitator agreed, "Yes, well, okay, then let's give Beth the floor," made me light-headed.

I practiced not apologizing. I remembered how I had apologized to Dick when he told me he didn't want me or any woman to work for him, as if it were somehow my fault. Saying "I'm sorry, I'm sorry" when I was guiltless caused a floppy

sensation in my whole body—as if my shoulders were droop-
ing, as if I'd become boneless—and I didn't want to do that to
myself anymore. A male business coach whom one of my
companies supplied to me told me that women say "I'm sorry"
too often. I started noticing that men rarely asked for anyone's
pardon. I wrote myself a note that said, "Don't apologize if you
didn't do anything wrong" and put it on my desk, clipped to a
small metal figure of a businesswoman in her suit and heels
with her black briefcase dangling from one hand. I took "sorry"
out of my work vocabulary, and it helped me grow stronger,
too, since I wasn't reinforcing the feeling that I had made a
mistake. I hadn't—it was just a bad habit. Instead of saying,
"Well, this probably isn't correct, and I'm sorry I don't have it
more fleshed out, but I think we should try another approach,"
I practiced at night taking out the weasel words and saying, "I
propose another approach."

Expressing our opinions and beliefs out loud where everyone can hear them is essential, but as we begin to raise gender
issues, our candor has consequences. At one of the companies I
worked for, there were, symbolically, the "fellows," and yes,
they were all fellows. Membership in this elite group was for
technologists who were visionary and who contributed con-
crete research results with both current and future impact. I
was determined that women needed and deserved to be part of
this group. I nominated Sharon, a strong woman with an
amazing track record. As I submitted the nomination, I got
pushback that she was too bossy, not a team player, and took
too much credit—which of course could have been said about
any of the current fellows. Those men all got there through
individual contributions—in fact, each man had to prove his
individual merit as part of his acceptance into the society. I
forged ahead with my recommendation, even without full sup-

port. Eventually, Sharon became a fellow, and an excellent one at that.

However, one man who opposed Sharon's nomination accused me of favoritism toward women and discrimination against men. He went to Human Resources and filed a complaint against me for discriminating against him and other men in the protected class of males over forty years of age. I suffered months of investigation and interrogation: "Why do you want Sharon as a fellow? Is she really qualified? Are you favoring women over men? Do you see yourself as a feminist?"

Commuting to and from work each day in bumper-to-bumper traffic, among drivers swerving to arrive at their offices or homes eight seconds faster, I roared, in the privacy of my old Prius, "Fuck you all!" at the injustice of this cross-examination. I pounded my fists on the steering wheel and tried not to swing off the road, though sometimes the thought of a few weeks' reprieve in the hospital sounded like a good idea.

The inquiry team interviewed my employees and scrutinized me until they couldn't uncover anything and closed the case. So, yes, there are consequences if we speak out. But Sharon is a fellow, and not only that—as of 2018, there are now two female fellows, and more to come in the future—so I crashed through a corporate ceiling.

I OFTEN FANTASIZE about how my life would have been different if my last name since birth, Jackson, had been, instead of "son of Jack," Jackdaughter or, better yet, Jilldaughter. What if I had escaped early from our patriarchal roots and possessed, in my own name, the visible existence of mothers and daughters in my past—a subtle name change as a major psychological shift? What would my life have been like if I hadn't been stuffed with negative messaging, humiliated, and harassed? I picture myself relaxed, confident, sleeping through the night peacefully with no screaming dreams. I don't have heart palpitations, gritted teeth, and a doctor-diagnosed case of temporomandibular joint dysfunction. I'm focused on science, my management skills, projects, and the business, because I'm not distracted and anxious, not spending hours and hours of each day trying to figure out what I'm going to do, say, combat, avoid, or ignore. I see myself formulating ideas, articulating the business case, winning my points because poor self-esteem isn't dragging me down.

At work, I'm more productive because I'm not spending time determined not to cry. I'm relaxed because none of my bosses is making up false rumors about my sexual activities. I'm confident because my coworkers see me as an important part of the team, not a sex object or an EEO obligation. I'm energetic because I don't have to fight the depression brought on by these humiliating incidents. I have an appetite and even gain a few pounds, instead of being boy-skinny, since my stomach is no longer in knots.

Increasing the number of women in tech fields and in corporations by eliminating sexist behaviors and harassment is a joint effort. The problem is a big, circular chain. Young girls are demeaned by a parent and develop an inferiority complex. Young boys are taught to be macho and sexist as they grow up. Reinforced at school by teachers and peers, girls further realize their lesser status and boys begin to see their advantage. In college, the plot thickens as gender harassment and discrimination become tools for keeping women out, especially in STEM fields. The use of these tools only increases at the corporate level, as the competition becomes fiercer. Women quit, leaving the power in the hands of men, who then control the world—not to mention also influencing how women feel about themselves and how their children turn out—and the chain spins around and around like one on an old, tired bicycle.

We've all contributed to the problem of female harassment and the lack of women in the man world—parents with their early childhood lessons, academia, corporate America, men and women. Men can help with the change by stopping any threatening and power-hungry behavior in the workplace and at home. Women can contribute by overcoming low self-esteem as best we can through counseling, positive thinking, speaking up, and supporting one another. Men and women alike can teach our daughters and sons to be kind and strong, to embrace both girl power and boy liberation. It's time to set aside our differences, make these changes today, and look toward tomorrow, where new definitions of strength and freedom await everyone. Let's leave sexism and sexual harassment where they belong—in the past.

epilogue

~)

FREEDOM

I HAVE NEVER FELT SO FREE. I LEFT THE CORPORATE SCENE IN 2016, and I now know what true liberation feels like. I don't have to have dinner with anyone I don't like, don't have to smile when I'm furious, don't have to laugh at a sex joke when it's not funny. I have not looked back once and said, "Oh, I miss the sexually harassing work world."

I'm sure countless refugees and retirees from company life wrap the freedom of this time of life around their bodies and sleep with it clutched to their chest at night, but the particular gift of this stage for me is that I can live from now on without any of the sexual harassment that I had to put up with just to survive. Now I don't have to swallow it, wash it down, and feel it roiling in my stomach all day in order to keep my job or protect myself from retaliation. I wish I could have felt this way when I was younger. I am hopeful for future women that they won't have to quit or retire to get away from sexual ha-rassment—that they can have just a regular workday with its usual trials.

I will never stop hoping for this evolution, but it has hit me that I may not see these goals reach fruition in my lifetime. In April 2018, when I was sixty-six years old, for Christ's sake, it happened again.

Most of my friends don't ski anymore, but I still like to go up to the mountains and speed down a run; enjoy the bracing air on my face; suck in the piney smell of the woods; hear the *whish-whish* through my ears, tucked inside my headband and helmet; get a full-body workout. I go by myself now; I don't mind skiing single, deliciously alone on the slope. I savor the time to think, and sometimes I head off the trail and just stand still among the conifers, look out at the view, and tingle with the freedom I so relish. But I'm not completely free.

As I shared the lift with two older men, probably around my age, I had to listen to one of them go on and on, blabbing to his buddy about his skiing prowess and how he's such a big mountain biker, which I doubted, judging by the size of his midsection. Brag, brag, brag—it was a long ride. Herds of older men ski during the week, and not many women, so there I was again, the lone female. I was glad to get off the chairlift and make my run. It was a good one, with fresh powder and sunshine, and at the bottom of the hill, I lined up again in the single lane, ready for another go.

I spotted a man standing close by, looking in my direction, as if he were waiting for me.

He gave me a long, inviting look, as if I were supposed to respond, and when I said, "Do I know you?" he replied, "I'm the guy on the lift who talks too much. I didn't get a chance to chat with you on the last ride."

I recognized him and said inside my head, *Yeah, that's because you were so busy yakking about yourself.*

"Let's ride up together," he proposed, and as we waited in line, he started in, "Well, last time I came up here, I was with a girlfriend and we got invited to stay at this friend's cabin. We go over there, and my friend shows up with his girlfriend and another couple, and they turn out to be into sex orgies—you know, threesomes and stuff like that. You should try it some-time. Are you into it? Let me tell you. . . ."

As he began to describe the scene, I sighed and said, "Stop right there. I'm not interested," then swung my eyes and body away. It's definitely easier now that I have self-confidence and I'm not in the work world, where I would have had to consider that he might make my professional life miserable or fire me. I ignored his grumbling—"Well, jeez, what's wrong with you?"—and, to make sure he didn't come after me again, I sidestepped out of line and greeted a new skier: "Want to ride up together?"

But it's disappointing for sure. Even late in my life, here was another man titillating himself by making a woman un-comfortable. It was still a power trip, maybe one of his last chances to be a dominant bully. It didn't wreck my week like it used to, but it weighed on my mind the next day as disgust crept into my head, along with those old feelings of *Why me? Why did he need to do that?* But this time, I could answer my own question: *It's not my fault, and I'm not to blame. He's a poor, insecure creep who never learned a different kind of masculinity. He needs BAML.* As I discussed it with my husband, he sug-gested spraying Mace in the guy's face. Maybe that's what it takes—a NIC (remember negative, immediate, and certain?) behavioral response to make old men just *stop* it.

Another recent development is that two of my harassers have contacted me. One sent me a friend request on Facebook, and the other invited me to connect on LinkedIn. Each time, when I saw their separate emails, I physically recoiled and walked out the door, down the street, with a scowl on my face and a stomp in my foot, and fumed for about twenty minutes.

I've analyzed these outreach efforts as three possible sce-narios. One, they just friended everyone and my name was on some list—a totally impersonal act. Two, they're clueless and oblivious and so absorbed by their egos that they don't even think anything happened. They were just playing around at work and had a fond memory of a young, perky girl long ago.

The first scenario elicits no reaction in me, but the second one is difficult to take, so I imagine a third scenario: They're afraid. They remember well how they bullied me and, thanks to #MeToo, fear for their safety. Their hope is that if they can reach out, be friendly, document that I wanted to be in contact with them, it all might lessen any inclination I have to name them. I hope it's the latter. I want them to be afraid.

While I loved the excitement of scientific discovery and the travel and all that I learned in the academic and working worlds, it's so good to have all this other crap behind me. But you can see that there are still repercussions. Damage was done.

Several times each week, I hustle into the dressing room of the local, Olympic-size pool, hang up my towel, strip off my clothes, wriggle into my one-piece Tyr swimsuit, spritz my hair before stuffing it into my silicone cap, adjust my goggles, and head outside to the pool deck. The *slap, slap, slap* of the other swimmers' arms against the water inspires me. I jump around, stretch, and breathe in the sweet, familiar smell of chlorine disinfectant as the morning breeze chills my skin.

"What's the water temperature today?" I ask the lifeguard up in his tall-legged chair, bundled up in a big blanket and oversize hooded coat.

"It's eighty," he says, removing the scarf over his face for a few seconds to answer me.

Okay, good. I can do that. There's steam wafting off the water—a positive sign. I plunge in and start my mile.

And then I take control of my brain, because if I don't, dark clouds will swirl into it.

I am peaceful. I am calm. I am beautiful. I am strong, I say inside my head, over and over, while I churn through the water—ten laps of free, ten of mixed breast and backstroke, ten of medley, fly, back, breast, free, on and on. It's my mantra to combat the many years when I thought the opposite: *I am anxious. I am scared. I am weak. I am helpless.*

It feels so good to be free, but I have to remind myself that I am.

When you do yoga, you're supposed to choose an "intention" or a mental image to bring focus to a quality you want to cultivate on and off your mat. For many, many years, twice a week, I rushed over to the on-site yoga studio from my office at lunchtime, pulled on my tights and tank top, and gave myself forty-five minutes of exercise and head space. The image in my mind was always a little deer. I know, it's laughable, really lame, but let me explain.

It's a fawn. It's alone. Sometimes it's all ragged, with twigs in its fur and sores on its body, and it's thin, ribs showing, hungry. It's me, of course—rampant symbolism.

I chose the deer for my yoga practice years ago; it bubbled up in me from childhood memories of the Disney movie *Bambi*. When I saw the film in the 1950s, it had a major impact on me because I identified with the young fawn. I understood how curious and lively Bambi was, always asking questions about nature the same way I was entranced and intrigued by polliwogs, spiders, flowers, and ponds. But I also related to Bambi in a dark way. He learned that there were dangers out there, "man with guns" (men with penises, via Freud, for me?), and he quivered with fright. In a harsh and food-shortage winter, the worst happened: Man shot and killed his mother, and—here's where I really started internalizing—Bambi was shocked, afraid, and alone. He ran through the dark woods, all innocence, calling for his mother. It was snowing heavily, cold; night was falling. He was helpless and small, his head hung low. This was me most of my life. No wonder I chose a deer as my mental image.

During my yoga practice, I tried to help and heal the deer —smoothing its coat, visualizing it prancing and tossing its head up in the air, until, by the end of *savasana*, it looked pretty good. However, at each subsequent session, I had to start over with the bedraggled little creature.

Now, my mental image for yoga is a big, strong mother deer. She's beautiful. She has battle scars, but she's good to go from the start, and during the practice I just watch her and delight in her. I'm working on my next, future intention, still with my doe. In a sunlit clearing among the oak forest, I see her proudly raise her head and look right at me, not distracted by an acorn woodpecker's *rat-a-tat* on the leathery bark of the trees. She holds her stare longer than I can; I'm the first one to blink. She turns away, moves slowly toward the brush, makes up her mind, and then darts off into the woods, on an urgent mission.

NOTES

INTRODUCTION

1. Equal Employment Opportunity Commission, "Charges Alleging Sex-Based Harassment (Charges Filed with EEOC), FY 2010–FY 2017," 2017.

2. Stephanie K. Johnson and Juan M. Madera, "Sexual Harassment Is Pervasive in the Restaurant Industry. Here's What Needs to Change," *Harvard Business Review*, January 18, 2018.

3. K. B. H. Clancy, R. G. Nelson, J. N. Rutherford, and K. Hinde, "Survey of Academic Field Experiences (SAFE): Trainees Report Harassment and Assault," *PLoS ONE* 9, no. 7 (July 2014).

4. Barbara Boxer, *The Art of Tough: Fearlessly Facing Politics and Life* (New York: Hachette Books, 2016), 76–78.

5. Chai R. Feldblum and Victoria A. Lipnic, "Select Task Force on the Study of Harassment in the Workplace," Equal Employment Opportunity Commission, June 2016.

6. Mary Karr, in conversation with the author, San Miguel Writers' Conference, San Miguel de Allende, Mexico, February 2017.

CHAPTER 1: HEAVY MESSAGES

1. The American Association of University Women Education Foundation, "How Schools Shortchange Girls," 1992.

2. Helen Cordes, "Raising Confident Girls," *Child*, September 2001.

3. Brian D. Johnson and Laurie Berdahl, "Will Your Boys Grow Up to Respect Women?" *Psychology Today*, February 25, 2018.

4. Olga Silverstein and Beth Rashbaum, *The Courage to Raise Good Men* (New York: Viking Penguin, 1994), 120–24.

5. Reva B. Siegel, "A Short History of Sexual Harassment," in Catharine A. MacKinnon and Reva B. Siegel, eds., *Directions in Sexual Harassment Law* (New Haven, CT: Yale University Press, 2004), 3–8.

6. Sascha Cohen, "A Brief History of Sexual Harassment in America Before Anita Hill," *Time,* April 11, 2016.

CHAPTER 2: KEEP US SILENT

1. L. Hinkelman, *The Girls' Index: New Insights into the Complex World of Today's Girls* (Columbus, OH: Ruling Our eXperiences, Inc., 2017), 27.

2. Lin Bian, Sarah-Jane Leslie, and Andrei Cimpian, "Gender Stereotypes About Intellectual Ability Emerge Early and Influence Children's Interests," *Science* 355, no. 6323 (January 2017): 389.

3. Mitra Toossi, "A Century of Change: The U.S. Labor Force, 1950-2050," *Monthly Labor Review*, May 2002.

4. Siegel, "A Short History of Sexual Harassment," 11, 20–21.

5. Helen Gurley Brown, *Sex and the Single Girl* (New York: Bernard Geis Associates, 1962), 89, 103.

6. Katharine Graham, *Personal History* (New York: Alfred A. Knopf, 1997), 416.

7. Boris Groysberg and Robin Abrahams, "Manage Your Work, Manage Your Life," *Harvard Business Review*, March 2014.

Chapter 3: Keep Us Down

1. Jennifer L. Berdahl, "Harassment Based on Sex: Protecting Social Status in the Context of Gender Hierarchy," *Academy of Management Review* 32, no. 2 (2007): 641–58.

2. L. F. Fitzgerald et al., "The Incidence and Dimensions of Sexual Harassment in Academia and the Workplace," *Journal of Vocational Behavior* 32 (1988): 152–75.

3. L. F. Fitzgerald, M. J. Gelfand, and F. Drasgow, "Measuring Sexual Harassment: Theoretical and Psychometric Advances," *Basic & Applied Social Psychology* 17 (1995): 425–45.

4. Bernice Yeung, *In a Day's Work: The Fight to End Sexual Violence Against America's Most Vulnerable Workers* (New York: The New Press, 2018), 5, 35–36.

5. Saru Jayaraman, *Forked: A New Standard for American Dining* (New York: Oxford University Press, 2016), 11–12.

6. Carrie Teejardin et al., "Doctors & Sex Abuse: Still Forgiven," *Atlantic Journal-Constitution*, July 6, 2016–April 26, 2018.

7. Shirley Chisholm, *Unbought and Unbossed* (Boston: Houghton Mifflin, 1970), xii, 164–68.

8. Graham, *Personal History*, 417–18.

9. Ibid., 425.

10. Lin Farley, *Sexual Shakedown: The Sexual Harassment of Women on the Job* (New York: McGraw-Hill, 1978), 90, 52–121.

Chapter 4: The Late '70s

1. CFI Group, "Technical Report: National Park Service (NPS) Work Environment Survey, January–March 2017," September 29, 2017.

2. Anita Hill, *Speaking Truth to Power* (New York: Doubleday, 1997), 195.

3. Jennifer L. Berdahl, "The Sexual Harassment of Uppity Women," *Journal of Applied Psychology*, 92, no. 2 (2007): 425–37.

4. Karen Sutherland, "Dating in the Workplace: Avoiding a Harassment Claim from a Relationship Gone Sour," January 2013, www.omwlaw.com/wp-content/uploads/2013/01/Dating-In-the-Workplace_-Avoiding-A-Harassment-Claim-From-A-Relationship-Gone-Sour.pdf.

5. Enid Nemy, "Women Begin to Speak Out Against Sexual Harassment at Work," *New York Times*, August 19, 1975.

6. Kaitlin Menza, "You Have to See Redbook's Shocking 1976 Sexual Harassment Survey," *Redbook*, November 28, 2016.

7. Sascha Cohen, "A Brief History of Sexual Harassment in America Before Anita Hill," *Time*, April 11, 2016.

8. Spencer Rich, "Schlafly: Sex Harassment on Job No Problem for Virtuous Women," *Washington Post*, April 22, 1981.

9. National Science Foundation, National Science Board Science & Engineering Indicators 2018, Chapter 3, "Science and Engineering Labor Force," January 2018.

10. Grace Donnelly, "Google's 2017 Diversity Report Shows Progress Hiring Women, Little Change for Minority Workers," *Fortune*, June 29, 2017.

CHAPTER 5: UPPING THE GAME

1. Amy Schumer, "Last Fuckable Day," *Inside Amy Schumer*, Season 3, April 21, 2015, www.comedycentral.co.uk/inside-amy-schumer/videos/inside-amy-schumer-last-fuckable-day.

2. Dante Chinni, "Poll: Views on Sexual Harassment at Work Divided Women by Age," *NBC News*, December 3, 2017, www.nbcnews.com/storyline/sexual-misconduct/poll-views-sexual-harassment-work-divide-women-age-n826011.

3. L. Berger and J. Waldfogel, "Maternity Leave and the Employment of New Mothers in the United States," *Journal of Population Economics* 17, no. 2 (June 2004): 331–49.

4. Jessica Deahl, "Countries Around the World Beat the US on Paid Parental Leave," NPR, *All Things Considered*, October 6, 2016, www.npr.org/2016/10/06/495839588/countries-around-the-world-beat-the-u-s-on-paid-parental-leave.

5. Kenneth M. York and Kelly J. Brookhouse, "The Legal History of Work-Related Sexual Harassment and Implications for Employers," *Employee Responsibilities and Rights Journal* 1, no. 3 (September 1988): 227–37.

6. Phyllis Schlafly, "The Power of the Positive Woman," (New York: Arlington House Publishers, 1977), 68–70.

CHAPTER 6: THE CORPORATE LADDER

1. Nicole Hemmer, "Hill Changed the Harassment Conversation," *U.S. News & World Report*, October 17, 2017.

2. Carol Kleiman, "Sexual Harassment Complaints on Rise," *Chicago Tribune*, March 7, 1992.

3. Marcia D. Greenberger, "What Anita Hill Did for America," CNN, October 22, 2010, www.cnn.com/2010/OPINION/10/21/greenberger.anita.hill/index.html.

4. Kevin McCoy, "Sexual Harassment: Here Are Some of the Biggest Cases," *USA Today*, October 25, 2017.

5. United States Court of Appeals, *Baldwin v. Blue Cross Blue Shield of Alabama*, no. 05-15619, March 19, 2007, https://caselaw.findlaw.com/us-11th-circuit/1002853.html.

CHAPTER 7: BOY CHILDREN

1. bell hooks, *The Will to Change: Men, Masculinity, and Love* (New York: Atria Books, 2004), 52.

2. Olga Silverstein and Beth Rashbaum, *The Courage to Raise Good Men* (New York: Penguin Books, 1994), 4–5, 27–32, 76, 235.

3. hooks, *The Will to Change*, 51.

4. David McGlynn, "In the #MeToo Era, Raising Boys to Be Good Guys," *New York Times,* June 1, 2018.

5. Alison Bowen, "Raising Boys Who Respect Women," *Chicago Tribune*, January 23, 2018.

6. Jennifer Newson, *The Mask You Live In*, the Representation Project, January 25, 2015, http://therepresentationproject.org/film/the-mask-you-live-in/.

7. Christia Spears Brown, *Parenting Beyond Pink and Blue: How to Raise Your Kids Free of Gender Stereotypes* (New York: Ten Speed Press, 2014), 85.

CHAPTER 8: THE CYCLE OF HARASSMENT

1. Harry Enten and Kathryn Casteel, "What Women Thought of Trump Through Year One," *FiveThirtyEight*, ABC News, January 22, 2018, https://fivethirtyeight.com/features/across-all-parties-ages-and-races-trump-is-less-popular-with-women-than-with-men/.

2. Andrea Park, "#MeToo Reaches 85 Countries with 1.7M Tweets," CBS News, October 24, 2017, www.cbsnews.com/news/metoo-reaches-85-countries-with-1-7-million-tweets/.

3. Nikki Graff, "Sexual Harassment at Work in the Era of #MeToo, Pew Research Center, April 4, 2018, www.pewsocial-trends.org/2018/04/04/sexual-harassment-at-work-in-the-era-of-metoo/.

4. Melanie Heenan and Suellen Murray, "Study of Reported Rapes in Victoria 2000-2003" (Melbourne, Victoria, Australia: Office of Women's Policy, 2006), 20.

5. D. Lisak, L. Gardinier, S. C. Nicksa, and A. M. Cote, "False Allegations of Sexual Assault: An Analysis of Ten Years of Reported Cases," *Violence Against Women* 12 (December 2010): 1318–34.

6. Kate Gilmore and Lise Pittman, "To Report or Not Report: A Study of Victims/Survivors of Sexual Assault and Their Experience of Making an Initial Report to the Police" (Carlton, Victoria, Australia: CASA House, 1993), 11–12.

7. Liz Kelly, "The (In)credible Words of Women: False Allegations in European Rape Research," *Violence Against Women* 12 (December 2010): 1372–74.

8. Liz Kelly, *Routes to (In)justice: A Research Review on the Reporting, Investigation and Prosecution of Rape Cases* (London: University of North London, 2001), 22–23, www.justiceinspectorates.-gov.uk/cjji/wp-content/uploads/sites/2/2014/04/Rapelitrev.pdf.

9. Lisa Lazard, "Here's the Truth About False Accusations of Sexual Violence," *Independent*, November 27, 2017.

10. Emily Chang, *Brotopia: Breaking Up the Boys' Club of Silicon Valley* (New York: Portfolio/Penguin, 2018), 6–7.

11. National Girls Collaborative Project, "Resources-Statistics-Stem Workforce," 2016, https://ngcproject.org/statistics.

12. Maeve Duggan, "Online Harassment," Pew Research Center, October 22, 2014, www.pewinternet.org/2014/10/22/online-harassment/.

13. Michael Kimmel, *Angry White Men: American Masculinity at the End of an Era* (New York: Nation Books, 2013), 284.

14. Michael Kimmel, *Manhood in America: A Cultural History* (New York: Oxford University Press, 2012), 297.

15. Alysse ElHage, "Boys in Crisis: An Interview with Warren Farrell," *Institute for Family Studies*, March 9, 2017, https://ifstudies.org/blog/boys-in-crisis-an-interview-with-warren-farrell.

16. Barbara Boxer, *The Art of Tough: Fearlessly Facing Politics and Life* (New York: Hachette Books, 2016), 3.

17. Hillary Rodham Clinton, *What Happened* (New York: Simon & Schuster, 2017), 147–48.

18. Condoleezza Rice, *Extraordinary, Ordinary People: A Memoir of Family* (New York: Three Rivers Press, 2011), 33.

19. Sheryl Sandberg, *Lean In: Women, Work and the Will to Lead* (New York: Alfred A. Knopf, 2013), 14.

20. Gretchen Carlson, *Be Fierce: Stop Harassment and Take Your Power Back* (New York: Center Street, 2017), 14.

21. "Data About Men Teachers: The Percentage of Male Teachers by Year in United States," MenTeach—U.S. Bureau of Data Statistics, 2017, www.menteach.org/resources/data_about_men_teachers.

22. "Traditional and Nontraditional Occupations," Women's Bureau, United States Department of Labor, 2014, www.dol.gov/wb/stats/nontra_traditional_occupations.htm.

23. Ariane Hegewisch and Emma Williams, "The Gender Wage Gap by Occupation 2017 and by Race and Ethnicity," Institute for Women's Policy Research, April 9, 2018, https://iwpr.org/publications/gender-wage-gap-occupation-2017-race-ethnicity/.

24. Claire Cain Miller, "Pink-Collar Work: Why Men Don't Want the Jobs Mostly Done by Women," *New York Times*, January 4, 2017.

25. Kimberly Lawson, "Why Many Men Would Rather Be Unemployed Than Do 'Women's Work,'" *Broadly*, January 6, 2017.

26. Carolyn Jones, "Girls Draw Even with Boys in High School STEM Classes, but Still Lag in College and Careers," *EdSource*, March 12, 2017.

27. Andrea Widener, "Sexual Harassment Pervasive in Science," *Chemical and Engineering News*, June 18, 2018.

28. National Academies of Sciences, Engineering, and Medicine, *Sexual Harassment of Women: Climate, Culture, and Consequences in Academic Sciences, Engineering, and Medicine* (Washington, DC: The National Academies Press, 2018), 67–91.

29. Jacklyn J. Ford, "Discrimination and Harassment Training Can Help Protect Employers," *Corporate Counsel Business Journal*, April 1, 2004.

CONCLUSION: STAY AND SPEAK UP

1. Yoni Blumberg, "Companies with More Female Executives Make More Money—Here's Why," CNBC, March 2, 2018, www.cnbc.com/2018/03/02/why-companies-with-female-managers-make-more-money.html.

2. Marcus Noland, Tyler Moran, and Barbara Kotschwar, "Is Gender Diversity Profitable? Evidence from a Global Survey," Peterson Institute for International Economics, February 2016,

https://piie.com/publications/working-papers/gender-diversity-profitable-evidence-global-survey.

3. Jenny M. Hoobler, et al., "The Business Case for Women Leaders: Meta-Analysis, Research Critique, and Path Forward," *Journal of Management* 44, no. 6 (March 2016): 2473–99.

4. Chang-Tai Hsieh, et al., "The Allocation of Talent and U.S. Economic Growth," Paris Institute of Political Studies, February 22, 2013, www.sciencespo.fr/newsletter/actu_medias/8466/erik-hurst.pdf.

5. Pat Wechsler, "Woman-Led Companies Perform Three Times Better Than the S&P 500," *Fortune*, March 3, 2015.

6. Gloria Steinem, in conversation with the author, East Bay Women's Conference, San Ramon, CA, March 2012.

ACKNOWLEDGMENTS

My sister, Deborah Jackson, and honorary sister, Linda Fisher, asked me for years to write this book. They could see how it would help others like us who have been harassed and discounted. They also thought it would make a great, though twisted, story—unbelievable to most people, who could never imagine that this much sexual harassment can happen to one female in our society. I love you both and hope this book meets your expectations.

Special thanks to Annie Tucker, an editor extraordinaire who made me a better writer while I couldn't even tell it was happening because we were having so many laughs and so much fun.

My friend Theresa Noe has kept me going since I first talked to her along that dusty pathway in Mexico. *Te quiero, mi amiga.*

Extra thanks and love to special women Gigi Arino, Silvia Garrigo, and Rochelle Lenahan for reading my first, very rough draft. Bonnie Cohn, Leah Eskenazi, Robin Jackson, Brian Kornow, Brittney Kornow, Katherine McCollough, Kaya Singer, Michelle Swanberg, and Jeff Wolinsky never failed to ask me, "How is your book coming along?" You don't know how much I appreciate your encouragement and friendship.

I cherish the many days those of us in Swathi Rajan's Shut Up and Write! group sat companionably side by side and wrote our hearts out. Your presence and support have been a mainstay and anchor for me.

Thank you to all the good men in my life who don't harass women. Special thanks to my best man friend and husband, Craig, who is always there for me, and to my three sons, who have become the wonderful men I knew they'd be.

ABOUT THE AUTHOR

Photo credit: Craig Hodges

LUCINDA JACKSON, a scientist and corporate executive, spent almost fifty years in academia and Fortune 500 companies. After growing up on the West Coast, she received her PhD in science and continued speaking and serving on boards of academic, nonprofit, and industry organizations worldwide. She has published peer-reviewed articles, patents, and book chapters and is working on a book series about freedom and breaking old patterns. After Peace Corps volunteerism in Palau and teaching science in Mexico, Jackson and her husband returned recently to their home near San Francisco. They have three liberated sons scattered around the globe.

SELECTED TITLES FROM SHE WRITES PRESS

She Writes Press is an independent publishing company
founded to serve women writers everywhere.
Visit us at www.shewritespress.com.

I'm Saying No! Standing Up Against Sexual Assault, Sexual Harassment, and Sexual Pressure by Beverly Engel. $16.95, 978-1631525254. In spite of the #MeToo and Time's Up movements, many women are still afraid to say no to unwanted sexual advances and reluctant to report sexual violations. Here, psychotherapist Engel offers a groundbreaking program to help all the women who have been silenced by past trauma or were raised to believe they didn't have a right to say no to stand up for themselves.

Stop Giving It Away: How to Stop Self-Sacrificing and Start Claiming Your Space, Power, and Happiness by Cherilynn Veland. $16.95, 978-1-63152-958-0. An empowering guide designed to help women break free from the trappings of the needs, wants, and whims of other people—and the self-imposed limitations that are keeping them from happiness.

In the Game: The Highs and Lows of a Trailblazing Trial Lawyer by Peggy Garrity. $16.95, 978-1-63152-105-8. Admitted to the California State Bar in 1975—when less than 3 percent of lawyers were women—Peggy Garrity refuses to choose between family and profession, and succeeds at both beyond anything she could have imagined.

Times They Were A-Changing: Women Remember the '60s & '70s edited by Kate Farrell, Amber Lea Starfire, and Linda Joy Myers. $16.95, 978-1-938314-04-9. Forty-eight powerful stories and poems detailing the breakthrough moments experienced by women during the '60s and '70s.

Transforming Knowledge: Public Talks on Women's Studies, 1976-2011 by Jean Fox O'Barr. $19.95, 978-1-938314-48-3. A collection of essays addressing one woman's challenges faced and lessons learned on the path to reframing—and effecting—feminist change.